Genghis Khan:
Makers of History Series

Illustrated Edition

By Jacob Abbott

ISBN#: 978-1-61104-004-3

Table of Contents

PREFACE

The word khan is not a name, but a title. It means chieftain or king. It is a word used in various forms by the different tribes and nations that from time immemorial have inhabited Central Asia, and has been applied to a great number of potentates and rulers that have from time to time arisen among them. Genghis Khan was the greatest of these princes. He was, in fact, one of the most renowned conquerors whose exploits history records.

As in all other cases occurring in the series of histories to which this work belongs, where the events narrated took place at such a period or in such a part of the world that positively reliable and authentic information in respect to them can now no longer be obtained, the author is not responsible for the actual truth of the narrative which he offers, but only for the honesty and fidelity with which he has compiled it from the best sources of information now within reach.

CHAPTER 1: PASTORAL LIFE IN ASIA

Four different modes of life enumerated—Northern and southern climes—Animal food in arctic regions—Tropical regions—Appetite changes with climate—First steps toward civilization—Interior of Asia—Pastoral habits of the people— Picture of pastoral life—Large families accumulated—Rise of patriarchal governments—Origin of the towns—Great chieftains—Genghis Khan.

There are four several methods by which the various communities into which the human race is divided obtain their subsistence from the productions of the earth, each of which leads to its own peculiar system of social organization, distinct in its leading characteristics from those of all the rest. Each tends to its own peculiar form of government, gives rise to its own manners and customs, and forms, in a word, a distinctive and characteristic type of life.

These methods are the following:

1. By hunting wild animals in a state of nature.
2. By rearing tame animals in pasturages.
3. By gathering fruits and vegetables which grow   spontaneously in a state of nature.
4. By rearing fruits and grains and other vegetables by   artificial tillage in cultivated ground.

By the two former methods man subsists on animal food. By the two latter on vegetable food.

As we go north, from the temperate regions toward the poles, man is found to subsist more and more on animal food. This seems to be the intention of Providence. In the arctic regions scarcely any vegetables grow that are fit for human food, but animals whose flesh is nutritious and adapted to the use of man are abundant.

As we go south, from temperate regions toward the equator, man is found to subsist more and more on vegetable food. This, too, seems to be the intention of nature. Within the tropics scarcely any animals live that are fit for human food; while fruits, roots, and other vegetable productions which are nutritious and adapted to the use of man are abundant.

In accordance with this difference in the productions of the different regions of the earth, there seems to be a difference in the constitutions of the races of men formed to inhabit them. The tribes that inhabit Greenland and Kamtschatka cannot preserve their accustomed health and vigor on any other than animal food. If put upon a diet of vegetables they soon begin to pine away. The reverse is true of the vegetable-eaters of the tropics. They preserve their health and strength well on a diet of rice, or bread-fruit, or bananas, and would undoubtedly be made sick by being fed on the flesh of walruses, seals, and white bears.

In the temperate regions the productions of the above-mentioned extremes are mingled. Here many animals whose flesh is fit for human food live and thrive, and here grows, too, a vast variety of nutritious fruits, and roots, and seeds. The physical constitution of the various races of men that inhabit these regions is modified accordingly. In the temperate climes men can live on vegetable food, or on animal food, or on both. The constitution differs, too, in different individuals, and it changes at different periods of the year. Some persons require more of animal, and others more of vegetable food, to preserve their bodily and mental powers in the best condition, and each one observes a change in himself in passing from winter to summer. In the summer the desire for a diet of fruits and vegetables seems to come northward with the sun, and in the winter the appetite for flesh comes southward from the arctic regions with the cold.

When we consider the different conditions in which the different regions of the earth are placed in respect to their capacity of production for animal and vegetable food, we shall see that this adjustment of the constitution of man, both to the differences of climate and to the changes of the seasons, is a very wise and beneficent arrangement of Divine Providence. To confine man absolutely either to animal or vegetable food would be to depopulate a large part of the earth.

It results from these general facts in respect to the distribution of the supplies of animal and vegetable food for man in different latitudes that, in all northern climes in our hemisphere, men living in a savage state must be hunters, while those that live near the equator must depend for their subsistence on fruits and roots growing wild. When, moreover, any tribe or race of men in either of these localities take the first steps toward civilization, they begin, in the one case, by taming animals, and rearing them in flocks and herds; and, in the other case, by saving the seeds of food-producing plants, and cultivating them by artificial tillage in enclosed and private fields. This last is the condition of all the half-civilized tribes of the tropical regions of the earth, whereas the former prevails in all the northern temperate and arctic regions, as far to the northward as domesticated animals can live.

From time immemorial, the whole interior of the continent of Asia has been inhabited by tribes and nations that have taken this one step in the advance toward civilization, but have gone no farther. They live, not, like the Indians in

North America, by hunting wild beasts, but by rearing and pasturing flocks and herds of animals that they have tamed. These animals feed, of course, on grass and herbage; and, as grass and herbage can only grow on open ground, the forests have gradually disappeared, and the country has for ages consisted of great grassy plains, or of smooth hill-sides covered with verdure. Over these plains, or along the river valleys, wander the different tribes of which these pastoral nations are composed, living in tents, or in frail huts almost equally movable, and driving their flocks and herds before them from one pasture-ground to another, according as the condition of the grass, or that of the springs and streams of water, may require.

We obtain a pretty distinct idea of the nature of this pastoral life, and of the manners and customs, and the domestic constitution to which it gives rise, in the accounts given us in the Old Testament of Abraham and Lot, and of their wanderings with their flocks and herds over the country lying between the Euphrates and the Mediterranean Sea. They lived in tents, in order that they might remove their habitations the more easily from place to place in following their flocks and herds to different pasture-grounds. Their wealth consisted almost wholly in these flocks and herds, the land being almost everywhere common. Sometimes, when two parties traveling together came to a fertile and well-watered district, their herdsmen and followers were disposed to contend for the privilege of feeding their flocks upon it, and the contention would often lead to a quarrel and combat, if it had not been settled by an amicable agreement on the part of the chieftains.

ENCAMPMENT OF A PATRIARCH.

The father of a family was the legislator and ruler of it, and his sons, with their wives, and his son's sons, remained with him, sometimes for many years, sharing his means of subsistence, submitting to his authority, and going with him from place to place, with all his flocks and herds. They employed, too, so many herdsmen, and other servants and followers, as to form, in many cases, quite an extended community, and sometimes, in case of hostilities with any other wandering tribe, a single patriarch could send forth from his own domestic circle a force of several hundred armed men. Such a company as this, when moving across the country on its way from one region of pasturage to another, appeared like an immense caravan on its march, and when settled at an encampment the tents formed quite a little town.

Whenever the head of one of these wandering families died, the tendency was not for the members of the community to separate, but to keep together, and allow the oldest son to take the father's place as chieftain and ruler. This was necessary for defense, as, of course, such communities as these were in perpetual danger of coming into collision with other communities roaming about like themselves over the same regions. It would necessarily result, too, from the circumstances of the case, that a strong and well-managed party, with an able and sagacious chieftain at the head of it, would attract other and weaker parties to join it; or, on the arising of some pretext for a quarrel, would make war upon it and conquer it. Thus, in process of time, small nations, as it were, would be formed, which would continue united and strong as long as the able leadership continued; and then they would separate into their original elements, which elements would be formed again into other combinations.

Such, substantially, was pastoral life in the beginning. In process of time, of course, the tribes banded together became larger and larger. Some few towns and cities were built as places for the manufacture of implements and arms, or as resting-places for the caravans of merchants in conveying from place to place such articles as were bought and sold. But these places were comparatively few and unimportant. A pastoral and roaming life continued to be the destiny of the great mass of the people. And this state of things, which was commenced on the banks of the Euphrates before the time of Abraham, spread through the whole breadth of Asia, from the Mediterranean Sea to the Pacific Ocean, and has continued with very little change from those early periods to the present time.

Of the various chieftains that have from time to time risen to command among these shepherd nations but little is known, for very few and very scanty records have been kept of the history of any of them. Some of them have been famous as conquerors, and have acquired very extended dominions. The most celebrated of all is perhaps Genghis Khan, the hero of this history. He came upon the stage more than three thousand years after the time of the great prototype of his class, the Patriarch Abraham.

CHAPTER 2: THE MONGULS

Monguls—Origin of the name—A Mongul family—Their occupations—Animals of the Monguls—Their towns and villages—Mode of building their tents—Bad fuel—Comfortless homes—Movable houses built at last—The painting—Account of a large movable house—The traveling chests—Necessity of such an arrangement—Houses in the towns—Roads over the plains—Tribes and families—Influence of diversity of pursuits—Tribes and clans—Mode of making war—Horsemen—The bow and arrow—The flying horseman—Nature of the bow and arrow—Superiority of fire-arms—Sources of information—Gog and Magog—Salam—Adventures of Salam and his party—The wonderful mountain—Great bolts and bars—The prisoners—Travelers' tales—Progress of intelligence.

Three thousand years is a period of time long enough to produce great changes, and in the course of that time a great many different nations and congeries of nations were formed in the regions of Central Asia. The term Tartars has been employed generically to denote almost the whole race. The Monguls are a portion of this people, who are said to derive their name from Mongol Khan, one of their earliest and most powerful chieftains. The descendants of this khan called themselves by his name, just as the descendants of the twelve sons of Jacob called themselves Israelites, or children of Israel, from the name Israel, which was one of the designations of the great patriarch from whose twelve sons the twelve tribes of the Jews descended. The country inhabited by the Monguls was called Mongolia.

To obtain a clear conception of a single Mongul family, you must imagine, first, a rather small, short, thick-set man, with long black hair, a flat face, and a dark olive complexion. His wife, if her face were not so flat and her nose so broad, would be quite a brilliant little beauty, her eyes are so black and sparkling. The children have much the appearance of young Indians as they run shouting among the cattle on the hill-sides, or, if young, playing half-naked about the door of the hut, their long black hair streaming in the wind.

Like all the rest of the inhabitants of Central Asia, these people depended almost entirely for their subsistence on the products of their flocks and herds. Of course, their great occupation consisted in watching their animals while feeding by day, and in putting them in places of security by night, in taking care of and rearing the young, in making butter and cheese from the milk, and clothing from the skins, in driving the cattle to and fro in search of pasturage, and, finally, in

11

making war on the people of other tribes to settle disputes arising out of conflicting claims to territory, or to replenish their stock of sheep and oxen by seizing and driving off the flocks of their neighbors.

The animals which the Monguls most prized were camels, oxen and cows, sheep, goats, and horses. They were very proud of their horses, and they rode them with great courage and spirit. They always went mounted in going to war. Their arms were bows and arrows, pikes or spears, and a sort of sword or sabre, which was manufactured in some of the towns toward the west, and supplied to them in the course of trade by great traveling caravans.

Although the mass of the people lived in the open country with their flocks and herds, there were, notwithstanding, a great many towns and villages, though such centres of population were much fewer and less important among them than they are in countries the inhabitants of which live by tilling the ground. Some of these towns were the residences of the khans and of the heads of tribes. Others were places of manufacture or centres of commerce, and many of them were fortified with embankments of earth or walls of stone.

The habitations of the common people, even those built in the towns, were rude huts made so as to be easily taken down and removed. The tents were made by means of poles set in a circle in the ground, and brought nearly together at the top, so as to form a frame similar to that of an Indian wigwam. A hoop was placed near the top of these poles, so as to preserve a round opening there for the smoke to go out. The frame was then covered with sheets of a sort of thick gray felt, so placed as to leave the opening within the hoop free. The felt, too, was arranged below in such a manner that the corner of one of the sheets could be raised and let down again to form a sort of door. The edges of the sheets in other places were fastened together very carefully, especially in winter, to keep out the cold air.

Within the tent, on the ground in the centre, the family built their fire, which was made of sticks, leaves, grass, and dried droppings of all sorts, gathered from the ground, for the country produced scarcely any wood. Countries roamed over by herds of animals that gain their living by pasturing on the grass and herbage are almost always destitute of trees. Trees in such a case have no opportunity to grow.

The tents of the Monguls thus made were, of course, very comfortless homes. They could not be kept warm, there was so much cold air coming continually in through the crevices, notwithstanding all the people's contrivances to make them tight. The smoke, too, did not all escape through the hoop-hole above. Much of it remained in the tent and mingled with the atmosphere. This evil was aggravated by the kind of fuel which they used, which was of such a nature that it made only a sort of smouldering fire instead of burning, like good dry wood, with a bright and clear flame.

The discomforts of these huts and tents were increased by the custom which prevailed among the people of allowing the animals to come into them, especially those that were young and feeble, and to live there with the family.

In process of time, as the people increased in riches and in mechanical skill, some of the more wealthy chieftains began to build houses so large and so handsome that they could not be conveniently taken down to be removed, and then they contrived a way of mounting them upon trucks placed at the four corners, and moving them bodily in this way across the plains, as a table is moved across a floor upon its castors. It was necessary, of course, that the houses should be made very light in order to be managed in this way. They were, in fact, still tents rather than houses, being made of the same materials, only they were put together in a more substantial and ornamental manner. The frame was made of very light poles, though these poles were fitted together in permanent joinings. The covering was, like that of the tents, made of felt, but the sheets were joined together by close and strong seams, and the whole was coated with a species of paint, which not only closed all the pores and interstices and made the structure very tight, but also served to ornament it; for they were accustomed, in painting these houses, to adorn the covering with pictures of birds, beasts, and trees, represented in such a manner as doubtless, in their eyes, produced a very beautiful effect.

These movable houses were sometimes very large. A certain traveler who visited the country not far from the time of Genghis Khan says that he saw one of these structures in motion which was thirty feet in diameter. It was drawn by twenty-two oxen. It was so large that it extended five feet on each side beyond the wheels. The oxen, in drawing it, were not attached, as with us, to the centre of the forward axle-tree, but to the ends of the axle-trees, which projected beyond the wheels on each side. There were eleven oxen on each side drawing upon the axle-trees. There were, of course, many drivers. The one who was chief in command stood in the door of the tent or house which looked forward, and there, with many loud shouts and flourishing gesticulations, issued his orders to the oxen and to the other men.

The household goods of this traveling chieftain were packed in chests made for the purpose, the house itself, of course, in order to be made as light as possible, having been emptied of all its contents. These chests were large, and were made of wicker or basket-work, covered, like the house, with felt. The covers were made of a rounded form, so as to throw off the rain, and the felt was painted over with a certain composition which made it impervious to the water.

These chests were not intended to be unpacked at the end of the journey, but to remain as they were, as permanent storehouses of utensils, clothing, and provisions. They were placed in rows, each on its own cart, near the tent, where they could be resorted to conveniently from time to time by the servants and attendants, as occasion might require. The tent placed in the centre, with these great chests on their carts near it, formed, as it were, a house with one great room standing by itself, and all the little rooms and closets arranged in rows by the side of it.

Some such arrangement as this is obviously necessary in case of a great deal of furniture or baggage belonging to a man who lives in a tent, and who desires to be at liberty to remove his whole establishment from place to place at short notice; for a tent, from the very principle of its construction, is incapable of being divided into rooms, or of accommodating extensive stores of furniture or goods. Of course, a special contrivance is required for the accommodation of this species of property. This was especially the case with the Monguls, among whom there were many rich and great men who often accumulated a large amount of movable property. There was one rich Mongul, it was said, who had two hundred such chest-carts, which were arranged in two rows around and behind his tent, so that his establishment, when he was encamped, looked like quite a little village.

The style of building adopted among the Monguls for tents and movable houses seemed to set the fashion for all their houses, even for those that were built in the towns, and were meant to stand permanently where they were first set up. These permanent houses were little better than tents. They consisted each of one single room without any subdivisions whatever. They were made round, too, like the tents, only the top, instead of running up to a point, was rounded like a dome. There were no floors above that formed on the ground, and no windows.

Such was the general character of the dwellings of the Monguls in the days of Genghis Khan. They took their character evidently from the wandering and pastoral life that the people led. One would have thought that very excellent roads would have been necessary to have enabled them to draw the ponderous carts containing their dwellings and household goods. But this was less necessary than might have been supposed on account of the nature of the country, which consisted chiefly of immense grassy plains and smooth river valleys, over which, in many places, wheels would travel tolerably well in any direction without much making of roadway. Then, again, in all such countries, the people who journey from place to place, and the herds of cattle that move to and fro, naturally fall into the same lines of travel, and thus, in time, wear great trails, as cows make paths in a pasture. These, with a little artificial improvement at certain points, make very good summer roads, and in the winter it is not necessary to use them at all.

The Monguls, like the ancient Jews, were divided into tribes, and these were subdivided into families; a family meaning in this connection not one household, but a large congeries of households, including all those that were of known relationship to each other. These groups of relatives had each its head, and the tribe to which they pertained had also its general head. There were, it is said, three sets of these tribes, forming three grand divisions of the Mongul people, each of which was ruled by its own khan; and then, to complete the system, there was the grand khan, who ruled over all.

A constitution of society like this almost always prevails in pastoral countries, and we shall see, on a little reflection, that it is natural that it should do so. In a country like ours, where the pursuits of men are so infinitely diversified, the descendants of different families become mingled together in the most promiscuous manner. The son of a farmer in one state goes off, as soon as he is of age, to some other state, to find a place among merchants or manufacturers, because he wishes to be a merchant or a manufacturer himself, while his father supplies his place on the farm perhaps by hiring a man who likes farming, and has come hundreds of miles in search of work. Thus the descendants of one American grandfather and grandmother will be found, after a lapse of a few years, scattered in every direction all over the land, and, indeed, sometimes all over the world.

It is the diversity of pursuits which prevails in such a country as ours, taken in connection with the diversity of capacity and of taste in different individuals, that produces this dispersion.

Among a people devoted wholly to pastoral pursuits, all this is different. The young men, as they grow up, can have generally no inducement to leave their homes. They continue to live with their parents and relatives, sharing the care of the flocks and herds, and making common cause with them in everything that is of common interest. It is thus that those great family groups are formed which exist in all pastoral countries under the name of tribes or clans, and form the constituent elements of the whole social and political organization of the people.

In case of general war, each tribe of the Monguls furnished, of course, a certain quota of armed men, in proportion to its numbers and strength. These men always went to war, as has already been said, on horseback, and the spectacle which these troops presented in galloping in squadrons over the plains was sometimes very imposing. The shock of the onset when they charged in this way upon the enemy was tremendous. They were armed with bows and arrows, and also with sabres. As they approached the enemy, they discharged first a shower of arrows upon him, while they were in the act of advancing at the top of their speed. Then, dropping their bows by their side, they would draw their sabres, and be ready, as soon as the horses fell upon the enemy, to cut down all opposed to them with the most furious and deadly blows.

If they were repulsed, and compelled by a superior force to retreat, they would gallop at full speed over the plains, turning at the same time in their saddles, and shooting at their pursuers with their arrows as coolly, and with as correct an aim, almost, as if they were still. While thus retreating the trooper would guide and control his horse by his voice, and by the pressure of his heels upon his sides, so as to have both his arms free for fighting his pursuers.

These arrows were very formidable weapons, it is said. One of the travelers who visited the country in those days says that they could be shot with so much force as to pierce the body of a man entirely through.

SHOOTING AT PURSUERS.

It must be remembered, however, in respect to all such statements relating to the efficiency of the bow and arrow, that the force with which an arrow can be thrown depends not upon any independent action of the bow, but altogether upon the strength of the man who draws it. The bow, in straightening itself for the propulsion of the arrow, expends only the force which the man has imparted to it by bending it; so that the real power by which the arrow is propelled is, after all, the muscular strength of the archer. It is true, a great deal depends on the qualities of the bow, and also on the skill of the man in using it, to make all this muscular strength effective. With a poor bow, or with unskillful management, a great deal of it would be wasted. But with the best possible bow, and with the most consummate skill of the archer, it is the strength of the archer's arm which throws the arrow, after all.

It is very different in this respect with a bullet thrown by the force of gunpowder from the barrel of a gun. The force in this case is the explosive force of the powder, and the bullet is thrown to the same distance whether it is a very weak man or a very strong man that pulls the trigger.

But to return to the Monguls. All the information which we can obtain in respect to the condition of the people before the time of Genghis Khan comes to us from the reports of travelers who, either as merchants, or as ambassadors from caliphs or kings, made long journeys into these distant regions, and have left records, more or less complete, of their adventures, and accounts of what they saw, in writings which have been preserved by the learned men of the East. It is very doubtful how far these accounts are to be believed. One of these travelers, a learned man named Salam, who made a journey far into the interior of Asia by order of the Calif Mohammed Amin Billah, sometime before the reign of Genghis Khan, says that, among other objects of research and investigation which occupied his mind, he was directed to ascertain the truth in respect to the two famous nations Gog and Magog, or, as they are designated in his account, Yagog and Magog. The story that had been told of these two nations by the Arabian writers, and which was extensively believed, was, that the people of Yagog were of the ordinary size of men, but those of Magog were only about two feet high. These people had made war upon the neighboring nations, and had destroyed many cities and towns, but had at last been overpowered and shut up in prison.

Salam, the traveler whom the calif sent to ascertain whether their accounts were true, traveled at the head of a caravan containing fifty men, and with camels bearing stores and provisions for a year. He was gone a long time. When he came back he gave an account of his travels; and in respect to Gog and Magog, he said that he had found that the accounts which had been heard respecting them were

17

true. He traveled on, he said, from the country of one chieftain to another till he reached the Caspian Sea, and then went on beyond that sea for thirty or forty days more. In one place the party came to a tract of low black land, which exhaled an odor so offensive that they were obliged to use perfumes all the way to overpower the noxious smells. They were ten days in crossing this fetid territory. After this they went on a month longer through a desert country, and at length came to a fertile land which was covered with the ruins of cities that the people of Gog and Magog had destroyed.

In six days more they reached the country of the nation by which the people of Gog and Magog had been conquered and shut up in prison. Here they found a great many strong castles. There was a large city here too, containing temples and academies of learning, and also the residence of the king.

The travelers took up their abode in this city for a time, and while they were there they made an excursion of two days' journey into the country to see the place where the people of Gog and Magog were confined. When they arrived at the place they found a lofty mountain. There was a great opening made in the face of this mountain two or three hundred feet wide. The opening was protected on each side by enormous buttresses, between which was placed an immense double gate, the buttresses and the gate being all of iron. The buttresses were surmounted with an iron bulwark, and with lofty towers also of iron, which were carried up as high as to the top of the mountain itself. The gates were of the width of the opening cut in the mountain, and were seventy-five feet high; and the valves, lintels, and threshold, and also the bolts, the lock, and the key, were all of proportional size.

Salam, on arriving at the place, saw all these wonderful structures with his own eyes, and he was told by the people there that it was the custom of the governor of the castles already mentioned to take horse every Friday with ten others, and, coming to the gate, to strike the great bolt three times with a ponderous hammer weighing five pounds, when there would be heard a murmuring noise within, which were the groans of the Yagog and Magog people confined in the mountain. Indeed, Salam was told that the poor captives often appeared on the battlements above. Thus the real existence of this people was, in his opinion, fully proved; and even the story in respect to the diminutive size of the Magogs was substantiated, for Salam was told that once, in a high wind, three of them were blown off from the battlements to the ground, and that, on being measured, they were found but three spans high.

This is a specimen of the tales brought home from remote countries by the most learned and accomplished travelers of those times. In comparing these absurd and ridiculous tales with the reports which are brought back from distant regions in our days by such travelers as Humboldt, Livingstone, and Kane, we shall perceive what an immense progress in intelligence and information the human mind has made since those days.

CHAPTER 3: YEZONKAI KHAN
1163-1175

Yezonkai Behadr—Orthography of Mongul names—Great diversities—Yezonkai's power—A successful warrior—Katay—The Khan of Temujin—Mongol custom—Birth of Genghis Khan—Predictions of the astrologer—Explanation of the predictions—Karasher—Education of Temujin—His precocity—His early marriage—Plans of Temujin's father—Karizu—Tayian—Death of Yezonkai.

The name of the father of Genghis Khan is a word which can not be pronounced exactly in English. It sounded something like this, _Yezonkai Behadr_, with the accent on the last syllable, Behadr, and the _a_ sounded like _a_ in _hark_. This is as near as we can come to it; but the name, as it was really pronounced by the Mongul people, cannot be written in English letters nor spoken with English sounds.

Indeed, in all languages so entirely distinct from each other as the Mongul language was from ours, the sounds are different, and the letters by which the sounds are represented are different too. Some of the sounds are so utterly unlike any sounds that we have in English that it is as impossible to write them in English characters as it is for us to write in English letters the sound that a man makes when he chirps to his horse or his dog, or when he whistles. Sometimes writers attempt to represent the latter sound by the word _whew_; and when, in reading a dialogue, we come to the word whew, inserted to express a part of what one of the speakers uttered, we understand by it that he whistled; but how different, after all, is the sound of the spoken word _whew_ from the whistling sound that it is intended to represent!

Now, in all the languages of Asia, there are many sounds as impossible to be rendered by the European letters as this, and in making the attempt every different writer falls into a different mode. Thus the first name of Genghis Khan's father is spelled by different travelers and historians, Yezonkai, Yesukay, Yessuki, Yesughi, Bissukay, Bisukay, Pisukay, and in several other ways. The real sound was undoubtedly as different from any of these as they were all different from each other. In this narrative I shall adopt the first of these methods, and call him Yezonkai Behadr.

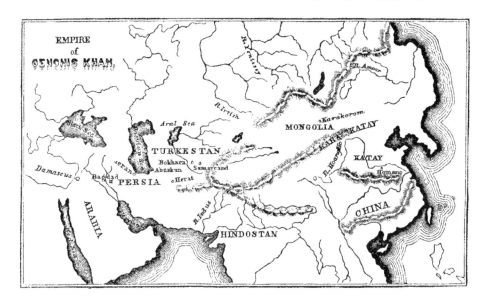

Yezonkai was a great khan, and he descended in a direct line through ten generations, so it was said, from a deity. Great sovereigns in those countries and times were very fond of tracing back their descent to some divine origin, by way of establishing more fully in the minds of the people their divine right to the throne. Yezonkai's residence was at a great palace in the country, called by a name, the sound of which, as nearly as it can be represented in English letters, was _Diloneldak_. From this, his capital, he used to make warlike excursions at the head of hordes of Monguls into the surrounding countries, in the prosecution of quarrels which he made with them under various pretexts; and as he was a skillful commander, and had great influence in inducing all the inferior khans to bring large troops of men from their various tribes to add to his army, he was usually victorious, and in this way he extended his empire very considerably while he lived, and thus made a very good preparation for the subsequent exploits of his son.

The northern part of China was at that time entirely separated from the southern part, and was under a different government. It constituted an entirely distinct country, and was called Katay.[A] This country was under the dominion of a chieftain called the Khan of Katay. This khan was very jealous of the increasing power of Yezonkai, and took part against him in all his wars with the tribes around him, and assisted them in their attempts to resist him; but he did not succeed. Yezonkai was too powerful for them, and went on extending his conquests far and wide.

[Footnote A: Spelled variously Kathay, Katay, Kitay, and in other ways.]

At last, under the pretense of some affront which he had received from them, Yezonkai made war upon a powerful tribe of Tartars that lived in his neighborhood. He invaded their territories at the head of an immense horde of Mongul troops, and began seizing and driving off their cattle.

The name of the khan who ruled over these people was Temujin. Temujin assembled his forces as soon as he could, and went to meet the invaders. A great battle was fought, and Yezonkai was victorious. Temujin was defeated and put to flight. Yezonkai encamped after the battle on the banks of the River Amoor, near a mountain. He had all his family with him, for it was often the custom, in these enterprises, for the chieftain to take with him not only all his household, but a large portion of his household goods. Yezonkai had several wives, and almost immediately after the battle, one of them, named Olan Ayka, gave birth to a son. Yezonkai, fresh from the battle, determined to commemorate his victory by giving his new-born son the name of his vanquished enemy. So he named him Temujin.[B] His birth took place, as nearly as can now be ascertained, in the year of our Lord 1163.

[Footnote B: The name is intended to be pronounced _Tim-oo-zhin_.]

Such were the circumstances of our hero's birth, for it was this Temujin who afterward became renowned throughout all Asia under the name of Genghis Khan. Through all the early part of his life, however, he was always known by the name which his father gave him in the tent by the river side where he was born.

Among the other grand personages in Yezonkai's train at this time, there was a certain old astrologer named Sugujin. He was a relative of Yezonkai, and also his principal minister of state. This man, by his skill in astrology, which he applied to the peculiar circumstances of the child, foretold for him at once a wonderful career. He would grow up, the astrologer said, to be a great warrior. He would conquer all his enemies, and extend his conquests so far that he would, in the end, become the Khan of all Tartary. Young Temujin's parents were, of course, greatly pleased with these predictions, and when, not long after this time, the astrologer died, they appointed his son, whose name was Karasher, to be the guardian and instructor of the boy. They trusted, it seems, to the son to give the young prince such a training in early life as should prepare him to realize the grand destiny which the father had foretold for him.

There would be something remarkable in the fact that these predictions were uttered at the birth of Genghis Khan, since they were afterward so completely fulfilled, were it not that similar prognostications of greatness and glory were almost always offered to the fathers and mothers of young princes in those days by the astrologers and soothsayers of their courts. Such promises were, of course, very flattering to these parents at the time, and brought those who made them into great favor. Then, in the end, if the result verified them, they were remembered and recorded as something wonderful; if not, they were forgotten.

Karasher, the astrologer's son, who had been appointed young Temujin's tutor, took his pupil under his charge, and began to form plans for educating him. Karasher was a man of great talents and of considerable attainments in learning, so far as there could be any thing like learning in such a country and among such a people. He taught him the names of the various tribes that lived in the countries around, and the names of the principal chieftains that ruled over them. He also gave him such information as he possessed in respect to the countries themselves, describing the situation of the mountains, the lakes, and the rivers, and the great deserts which here and there intervened between the fertile regions. He taught him, moreover, to ride, and trained him in all such athletic exercises as were practiced by the youth of those times. He instructed him also in the use of arms, teaching him how to shoot with a bow and arrow, and how to hold and handle his sabre, both when on horseback and when on foot. He particularly instructed him in the art of shooting his arrow in any direction when riding at a gallop upon his horse, behind as well as before, and to the right side as well as to the left. To do this coolly, skillfully, and with a true aim, required great practice as well as much courage and presence of mind.

Young Temujin entered into all these things with great spirit. Indeed, he very soon ceased to feel any interest in anything else, so that by the time that he was nine years of age it was said that he thought of nothing but exercising himself in the use of arms.

Nine years of age, however, with him was more than it would be with a young man among us, for the Asiatics arrive at maturity much earlier than the nations of Western Europe and America. Indeed, by the time that Temujin was thirteen years old, his father considered him a man—at least he considered him old enough to be married. He was married, in fact, and had two children before he was fifteen, if the accounts which the historians have given us respecting him are true.

Just before Temujin was thirteen, his father, in one of his campaigns in Katay, was defeated in a battle, and, although a great many of his followers escaped, he himself was surrounded and overpowered by the horsemen of the enemy, and was made prisoner. He was put under the care of a guard; for, of course, among people living almost altogether on horseback and in tents, there could be very few prisons. Yezonkai followed the camp of his conqueror for some time under the custody of his guard; but at length he succeeded in bribing his keeper to let him escape, and so contrived, after encountering many difficulties and suffering many hardships, to make his way back to his own country.

He was determined now to make a new incursion into Katay, and that with a larger force than he had had before. So he made an alliance with the chieftain of a neighboring tribe, called the Naymans; and, in order to seal and establish this alliance, he contracted that his son should marry the daughter of his ally. This was the time when Temujin was but thirteen years old. The name of this his first wife was Karizu—at least that was one of her names. Her father's name was Tayian.

Before Yezonkai had time to mature his plans for his new invasion of Katay, he fell sick and died. He left five sons and a daughter, it is said; but Temujin seems to have been the oldest of them all, for by his will his father left his kingdom, if the command of the group of tribes which were under his sway can be called a kingdom, to him, notwithstanding that he was yet only thirteen years old.

CHAPTER 4: THE FIRST BATTLE
1175

Temujin's accession—Discontent—Taychot and Chamuka—Arrangements for the battle—Temujin's ardor—Porgie—Exaggerated statements—The battle—Bravery of Temujin and Porgie—Influence of Temujin's example—Taychot slain—The victory—Rewards and honors—Temujin's rising fame—His second wife—Purta carried away captive—Customary present—Purta and Vang Khan—Purta's return—Birth of her child—Jughi—Temujin's wonderful dream—Disaffection among his subjects—A rebellion—Temujin discouraged—Temujin plans a temporary abdication—Arrangement of a regency—Temujin's departure.

In the language of the Monguls and of their neighbors the Tartars, a collection of tribes banded together under one chieftain was designated by a name which sounded like the word _orda_. This is the origin, it is said, of the English word _horde_.

The orda over which Yezonkai had ruled, and the command of which, at his death, he left to his son, consisted of a great number of separate tribes, each of which had its own particular chieftain. All these subordinate chieftains were content to be under Yezonkai's rule and leadership while he lived. He was competent, they thought, to direct their movements and to lead them into battle against their enemies. But when he died, leaving only a young man thirteen years of age to succeed him, several of them were disposed to rebel. There were two of them, in particular, who thought that they were themselves better qualified to reign over the nation than such a boy; so they formed an alliance with each other, and with such other tribes as were disposed to join them, and advanced to make war upon Temujin at the head of a great number of squadrons of troops, amounting in all to thirty thousand men.

The names of the two leaders of this rebellion were Taychot and Chamuka.

Young Temujin depended chiefly on his mother for guidance and direction in this emergency. He was himself very brave and spirited; but bravery and spirit, though they are of such vital importance in a commander on the field of battle, when the contest actually comes on, are by no means the principal qualities that are required in making the preliminary arrangements.

Accordingly, Temujin left the forming of the plans to his mother, while he thought only of his horses, of his arms and equipments, and of the fury with which he would gallop in among the enemy when the time should arrive for the battle to begin. His mother, in connection with the chief officers of the army and counselors of state who were around her, and on whom her husband Yezonkai, during his lifetime, had been most accustomed to rely, arranged all the plans. They sent off messengers to the heads of all the tribes that they supposed would be friendly to Temujin, and appointed places of rendezvous for the troops that they were to send. They made arrangements for the stores of provisions which would be required, settled questions of precedence among the different clans, regulated the order of march, and attended to all other necessary details.

In the mean time, Temujin thought only of the approaching battle. He was engaged continually in riding up and down upon spirited horses, and shooting in all directions, backward and forward, and both to the right side and to the left, with his bow and arrow. Nor was all this exhibition of ardor on his part a mere useless display. It had great influence in awakening a corresponding ardor among the chieftains of the troops, and among the troops themselves. They felt proud of the spirit and energy which their young prince displayed, and were more and more resolved to exert themselves to the utmost in defending his cause.

There was another young prince, of the name of Porgie, of about Temujin's age, who was also full of ardor for the fight. He was the chieftain of one of the tribes that remained faithful to Temujin, and he was equally earnest with Temujin for the battle to begin.

At length the troops were ready, and, with Temujin and his mother at the head of them, they went forth to attack the rebels. The rebels were ready to receive them. They were thirty thousand strong, according to the statements of the historians. This number is probably exaggerated, as all numbers were in those days, when there was no regular enrollment of troops and no strict system of enumeration.

At any rate, there was a very great battle. Immense troops of horsemen coming at full speed in opposite directions shot showers of arrows at each other when they arrived at the proper distance for the arrows to take effect, and then, throwing down their bows and drawing their sabres, rushed madly on, until they came together with an awful shock, the dreadful confusion and terror of which no person can describe. The air was filled with the most terrific outcries, in which yells of fury, shrieks of agony, and shouts of triumph were equally mingled. Some of the troops maintained their position through the shock, and rode on, bearing down all before them. Others were overthrown and trampled in the dust; while all, both those who were up and those who were down, were cutting in every direction with their sabres, killing men and inciting the horses to redoubled fury by the wounds which they gave them.

In the midst of such scenes as these Temujin and Porgie fought furiously with the rest. Temujin distinguished himself greatly. It is probable that those who were immediately around him felt that he was under their charge, and that they must do all in their power to protect him from danger. This they could do much more easily and effectually under the mode of fighting which prevailed in those days than would be possible now, when gunpowder is the principal agent of destruction. Temujin's attendants and followers could gather around him and defend him from assailants. They could prevent him from charging any squadron which was likely to be strong enough to overpower him, and they could keep his enemies so much at bay that they could not reach him with their sabres. But upon a modern field of battle there is much less opportunity to protect a young prince or general's son, or other personage whose life may be considered as peculiarly valuable. No precautions of his attendants can prevent a bomb's bursting at his feet, or shield him from the rifle balls that come whistling from such great distances through the air.

At any rate, whether protected by his attendants or only by the fortune of war, Temujin passed through the battle without being hurt, and the courage and energy which he displayed were greatly commended by all who witnessed them. His mother was in the battle too, though, perhaps, not personally involved in the actual conflicts of it. She directed the manoeuvres, however, and by her presence and her activity greatly encouraged and animated the men. In consequence of the spirit and energy infused into the troops by her presence, and by the extraordinary ardor and bravery of Temujin, the battle was gained. The army of the enemy was put to flight. One of the leaders, Taychot, was slain. The other made his escape, and Temujin and his mother were left in possession of the field.

Of course, after having fought with so much energy and effect on such a field, Temujin was now no longer considered as a boy, but took his place at once as a man among men, and was immediately recognized by all the army as their prince and sovereign, and as fully entitled, by his capacity if not by his years, to rule in his own name. He assumed and exercised his powers with as much calmness and self-possession as if he had been accustomed to them for many years. He made addresses to his officers and soldiers, and distributed honors and rewards to them with a combined majesty and grace which, in their opinion, denoted much grandeur of soul. The rewards and honors were characteristic of the customs of the country and the times. They consisted of horses, arms, splendid articles of dress, and personal ornaments. Of course, among a people who lived, as it were, always on horseback, such objects as these were the ones most highly prized.

The consequence of this victory was, that nearly the whole country occupied by the rebels submitted without any farther resistance to Temujin's sway. Other tribes, who lived on the borders of his dominions, sent in to propose treaties of alliance. The khan of one of these tribes demanded of Temujin the hand of his sister in marriage to seal and confirm the alliance which he proposed to make. In a word, the fame of Temujin's prowess spread rapidly after the battle over all the surrounding countries, and high anticipations began to be formed of the greatness and glory of his reign.

In the course of the next year Temujin was married to his second wife, although he was at this time only fourteen years old. The name of his bride was Purta Kugin. By this wife, who was probably of about his own age, he had a daughter, who was born before the close of the year after the marriage.

In his journeys about the country Temujin sometimes took his wives with him, and sometimes he left them temporarily in some place of supposed security. Toward the end of the second year Purta was again about to become a mother, and Temujin, who at that time had occasion to go off on some military expedition, fearing that the fatigue and exposure would be more than she could well bear, left her at home. While he was gone a troop of horsemen, from a tribe of his enemies, came suddenly into the district on a marauding expedition. They overpowered the troops Temujin had left to guard the place, and seized and carried off everything that they could find that was valuable. They made prisoner of Purta, too, and carried her away a captive. The plunder they divided among themselves, but Purta they sent as a present to a certain khan who reigned over a neighboring country, and whose favor they wished to secure. The name of this chieftain was Vang Khan. As this Vang Khan figures somewhat conspicuously in the subsequent history of Temujin, a full account of him will be given in the next chapter. All that is necessary to say here is, that the intention of the captors of Purta, in sending her to him as a present, was that he should make her his wife. It was the custom of these khans to have as many wives as they could obtain, so that when prisoners of high rank were taken in war, if there were any young and beautiful women among them, they were considered as charming presents to send to any great prince or potentate near, whom the captors were desirous of pleasing. It made no difference, in such cases, whether the person who was to receive the present were young or old. Sometimes the older he was the more highly he would prize such a gift.

Vang Khan, it happened, was old. He was old enough to be Temujin's father. Indeed, he had been in the habit of calling Temujin his son. He had been in alliance with Yezonkai, Temujin's father, some years before, when Temujin was quite a boy, and it was at that time that he began to call him his son.

PURTA IN THE TENT OF VANG KAHN.

Accordingly, when Purta was brought to him by the messengers who had been sent in charge of her, and presented to him in his tent, he said,

"She is very beautiful, but I cannot take her for my wife, for she is the wife of my son. I cannot marry the wife of my son."

Vang Khan, however, received Purta under his charge, gave her a place in his household, and took good care of her.

When Temujin returned home from his expedition, and learned what had happened during his absence, he was greatly distressed at the loss of his wife. Not long afterward he ascertained where she was, and he immediately sent a deputation to Vang Khan asking him to send her home. With this request Vang Khan immediately complied, and Purta set out on her return. She was stopped on the way, however, by the birth of her child. It was a son. As soon as the child was born it was determined to continue the journey, for there was danger, if they delayed, that some new troop of enemies might come up, in which case Purta would perhaps be made captive again. So Purta, it is said, wrapped up the tender limbs of the infant in some sort of paste or dough, to save them from the effects of the jolting produced by the rough sort of cart in which she was compelled to ride, and in that condition she held the babe in her lap all the way home.

She arrived at her husband's residence in safety. Temujin was overjoyed at seeing her again; and he was particularly pleased with his little son, who came out of his packing safe and sound. In commemoration of his safe arrival after so strange and dangerous a journey, his father named him Safe-arrived; that is, he gave him for a name the word in their language that means that. The word itself was Jughi.

The commencement of Temujin's career was thus, on the whole, quite prosperous, and everything seemed to promise well. He was himself full of ambition and of hope, and began to feel dissatisfied with the empire which his father had left him, and to form plans for extending it. He dreamed one night that his arms grew out to an enormous length, and that he took a sword in each of them, and stretched them out to see how far they would reach, pointing one to the eastward and the other to the westward. In the morning he related his dream to his mother. She interpreted it to him. She told him it meant undoubtedly that he was destined to become a great conqueror, and that the directions in which his kingdom would be extended were toward the eastward and toward the westward.

Temujin continued for about two years after this in prosperity, and then his good fortune began to wane. There came a reaction. Some of the tribes under his dominion began to grow discontented. The subordinate khans began to form plots and conspiracies. Even his own tribe turned against him. Rebellions broke out in various parts of his dominions; and he was obliged to make many hurried expeditions here and there, and to fight many desperate battles to suppress them. In one of these contests he was taken prisoner. He, however, contrived to make his escape. He then made proposals to the disaffected khans, which he hoped would satisfy them, and bring them once more to submit to him, since what he thus offered to do in these proposals was pretty much all that they had professed to require. But the proposals did not satisfy them. What they really intended to do was to depose Temujin altogether, and then either divide his dominions among themselves, or select some one of their number to reign in his stead.

At last, Temujin, finding that he could not pacify his enemies, and that they were, moreover, growing stronger every day, while those that adhered to him were growing fewer in numbers and diminishing in strength, became discouraged. He began to think that perhaps he really was too young to rule over a kingdom composed of wandering hordes of men so warlike and wild, and he concluded for a time to give up the attempt, and wait until times should change, or, at least, until he should be grown somewhat older. Accordingly, in conjunction with his mother, he formed a plan for retiring temporarily from the field; unless, indeed, as we might reasonably suspect, his mother formed the plan herself, and by her influence over him induced him to adopt it.

The plan was this: that Temujin should send an ambassador to the court of Vang Khan to ask Vang Khan to receive him, and protect him for a time in his dominions, until the affairs of his own kingdom should become settled. Then, if

Vang Khan should accede to this proposal, Temujin was to appoint his uncle to act as regent during his absence. His mother, too, was to be married to a certain emir, or prince, named Menglik, who was to be made prime minister under the regent, and was to take precedence of all the other princes or khans in the kingdom. The government was to be managed by the regent and the minister until such time as it should be deemed expedient for Temujin to return.

This plan was carried into effect. Vang Khan readily consented to receive Temujin into his dominions, and to protect him there. He was very ready to do this, he said, on account of the friendship which he had borne for Temujin's father. Temujin's mother was married to the emir, and the emir was made the first prince of the realm. Finally, Temujin's uncle was proclaimed regent, and duly invested with all necessary authority for governing the country until Temujin's return. These things being all satisfactorily arranged, Temujin set out for the country of Vang Khan at the head of an armed escort, to protect him on the way, of six thousand men. He took with him all his family, and a considerable suite of servants and attendants. Among them was his old tutor and guardian Karasher, the person who had been appointed by his father to take charge of him, and to teach and train him when he was a boy.

Being protected by so powerful an escort, Temujin's party were not molested on their journey, and they all arrived safely at the court of Vang Khan.

CHAPTER 5: VANG KHAN
1175

Karakatay—Vang Khan's dominions—The cruel fate of Mergus—His wife's stratagem—Nawr—He falls into the snare—Armed men in ambuscade—Death of Nawr—Credibility of these tales—Early life of Vang Khan—Reception of Temujin—Prester John—His letter to the King of France—Other letters—The probable truth—Temujin and Vang Khan.

The country over which Vang Khan ruled was called Karakatay. It bordered upon the country of Katay, which has already been mentioned as forming the northern part of what is now China. Indeed, as its name imports, it was considered in some sense as a portion of the same general district of country. It was that part of Katay which was inhabited by Tartars.

Vang Khan's name at first was Togrul. The name Vang Khan, which was, in fact, a title rather than a name, was given him long afterward, when he had attained to the height of his power. To avoid confusion, however, we shall drop the name Togrul, and call him Vang Khan from the beginning.

Vang Khan was descended from a powerful line of khans who had reigned over Karakatay for many generations. These khans were a wild and lawless race of men, continually fighting with each other, both for mastery, and also for the plunder of each other's flocks and herds. In this way most furious and cruel wars were often fought between near relatives. Vang Khan's grandfather, whose name was Mergus, was taken prisoner in one of these quarrels by another khan, who, though he was a relative, was so much exasperated by something that Mergus had done that he sent him away to a great distance to the king of a certain country which is called Kurga, to be disposed of there. The King of Kurga put him into a sack, sewed up the mouth of it, and then laid him across the wooden image of an ass, and left him there to die of hunger and suffocation.

The wife of Mergus was greatly enraged when she heard of the cruel fate of her husband. She determined to be revenged. It seems that the relative of her husband who had taken him prisoner, and had sent him to the King of Kurga, had been her lover in former times before her marriage; so she sent him a message, in which she dissembled her grief for the loss of her husband, and only blamed the King of Kurga for his cruel death, and then said that she had long felt an affection for him, and that, if he continued of the same mind as when he had formally addressed her, she was now willing to become his wife, and offered, if he would come to a certain place, which she specified, to meet her, she would join him there.

Nawr, for that was the chieftain's name, fell at once into the snare which the beautiful widow thus laid for him. He immediately accepted her proposals, and proceeded to the place of rendezvous. He went, of course, attended by a suitable guard, though his guard was small, and consisted chiefly of friends and personal attendants. The princess was attended also by a guard, not large enough, however, to excite any suspicion. She also took with her in her train a large number of carts, which were to be drawn by bullocks, and which were laden with stores of provisions, clothing, and other such valuables, intended as a present for her new husband. Among these, however, there were a large number of great barrels, or rounded receptacles of some sort, in which she had concealed a considerable force of armed men. These receptacles were so arranged that the men concealed in them could open them from within in an instant, at a given signal, and issue forth suddenly all armed and ready for action.

Among the other stores which the princess had provided, there was a large supply of a certain intoxicating drink which the Monguls and Tartars were accustomed to make in those days. As soon as the two parties met at the place of rendezvous the princess gave Nawr a very cordial greeting, and invited him and all his party to a feast, to be partaken on the spot. The invitation was accepted, the stores of provisions were opened, and many of the presents were unpacked and displayed. At the feast Nawr and his party were all supplied abundantly with the intoxicating liquor, which, as is usual in such cases, they were easily led to drink to excess; while, on the other hand, the princess's party, who knew what was coming, took good care to keep themselves sober. At length, when the proper moment arrived, the princess made the signal. In an instant the men who had been placed in ambuscade in the barrels burst forth from their concealment and rushed upon the guests at the feast. The princess herself, who was all ready for action, drew a dagger from her girdle and stabbed Nawr to the heart. Her guards, assisted by the re-enforcement which had so suddenly appeared, slew or secured all his attendants, who were so totally incapacitated, partly by the drink which they had taken, and partly by their astonishment at the sudden appearance of so overwhelming a force, that they were incapable of making any resistance.

The princess, having thus accomplished her revenge, marshaled her men, packed up her pretended presents, and returned in triumph home.

Such stories as these, related by the Asiatic writers, though they were probably often much embellished in the narration, had doubtless all some foundation in fact, and they give us some faint idea of the modes of life and action which prevailed among these half-savage chieftains in those times. Vang

Khan himself was the grandson of Mergus, who was sewed up in the sack. His father was the oldest son of the princess who contrived the above-narrated stratagem to revenge her husband's death. It is said that he used to accompany his father to the wars when he was only ten years old. The way in which he formed his friendship for Yezonkai, and the alliance with him which led him to call Temujin his son and to refuse to take his wife away from him, as already related, was this: When his father died he succeeded to the command, being the oldest son; but the others were jealous of him, and after many and long quarrels with them and with other relatives, especially with his uncle, who seemed to take the lead against him, he was at last overpowered or outmanoeuvred, and was obliged to fly. He took refuge, in his distress, in the country of Yezonkai. Yezonkai received him in a very friendly manner, and gave him effectual protection. After a time he furnished him with troops, and helped him to recover his kingdom, and to drive his uncle away into banishment in his turn. It was while he was thus in Yezonkai's dominions that he became acquainted with Temujin, who was then very small, and it was there that he learned to call him his son. Of course, now that Temujin was obliged to fly himself from his native country and abandon his hereditary dominions, as he had done before, he was glad of the opportunity of requiting to the son the favor which he had received, in precisely similar circumstances, from the father, and so he gave Temujin a very kind reception.

There is another circumstance which is somewhat curious in respect to Vang Khan, and that is, that he is generally supposed to be the prince whose fame was about this period spread all over Europe, under the name of Prester John, by the Christian missionaries in Asia. These missionaries sent to the Pope, and to various Christian kings in Europe, very exaggerated accounts of the success of their missions among the Persians, Turks, and Tartars; and at last they wrote word that the great Khan of the Tartars had become a convert, and had even become a preacher of the Gospel, and had taken the name of Prester John. The word _prester_ was understood to be a corruption of presbyter. A great deal was accordingly written and said all through Christendom about the great Tartar convert, Prester John. There were several letters forwarded by the missionaries, professedly from him, and addressed to the Pope and to the different kings of Europe. Some of these letters, it is said, are still in existence. One of them was to the King of France. In this letter the writer tells the King of France of his great wealth and of the vastness of his dominions. He says he has seventy kings to serve and wait upon him. He invites the King of France to come and see him, promising to bestow a great kingdom upon him if he will, and also to make him his heir and leave all his dominions to him when he dies; with a great deal more of the same general character.

The other letters were much the same, and the interest which they naturally excited was increased by the accounts which the missionaries gave of the greatness and renown of this more than royal convert, and of the progress which Christianity had made and was still making in his dominions through their instrumentality.

It is supposed, in modern times, that these stories were pretty much all inventions on the part of the missionaries, or, at least, that the accounts which they sent were greatly exaggerated and embellished; and there is but little doubt that they had much more to do with the authorship of the letters than any khan. Still, however, it is supposed that there was a great prince who at least encouraged the missionaries in their work, and allowed them to preach Christianity in his dominions, and, if so, there is little doubt that Vang Khan was the man.

At all events, he was a very great and powerful prince, and he reigned over a wide extent of country. The name of his capital was Karakorom. The distance which Temujin had to travel to reach this city was about ten days' journey.

He was received by Vang Khan with great marks of kindness and consideration. Vang Khan promised to protect him, and, in due time, to assist him in recovering his kingdom. In the mean while Temujin promised to enter at once into Vang Khan's service, and to devote himself faithfully to promoting the interests of his kind protector by every means in his power.

CHAPTER 6: TEMUJIN IN EXILE
1182

*Temujin's popularity—Rivals and enemies appear—Plots—Yemuka—
Wisulujine—Yemuka's disappointment—His rage—Conspiracy formed—
Progress of the league—Oath of the conspirators—The oath—Karakorom—Plan
formed by Temujin—The campaign—Unexpected arrival of Vang Khan—His
story—Temujin's promises—Result of the battle—Temujin victorious—State of
things at Karakorom—Erkekara—Preparations for the final conflict—Erkekara
vanquished—Vang Khan restored—Temujin's popularity.*

Vang Khan gave Temujin a very honorable position in his court. It was
natural that he should do so, for Temujin was a prince in the prime of his youth,
and of very attractive person and manners; and, though he was for the present an
exile, as it were, from his native land, he was not by any means in a destitute or
hopeless condition. His family and friends were still in the ascendency at home,
and he himself, in coming to the kingdom of Vang Khan, had brought with him
quite an important body of troops. Being, at the same time, personally possessed
of great courage and of much military skill, he was prepared to render his
protector good service in return for his protection. In a word, the arrival of
Temujin at the court of Vang Khan was an event calculated to make quite a
sensation.

At first everybody was very much pleased with him, and he was very popular;
but before long the other young princes of the court, and the chieftains of the
neighboring tribes, began to be jealous of him. Vang Khan gave him precedence
over them all, partly on account of his personal attachment to him, and partly on
account of the rank which he held in his own country, which, being that of a
sovereign prince, naturally entitled him to the very highest position among the
subordinate chieftains in the retinue of Vang Khan. But these subordinate
chieftains were not satisfied. They murmured, at first secretly, and afterward
more openly, and soon began to form combinations and plots against the new
favorite, as they called him.

An incident soon occurred which greatly increased this animosity, and gave to
Temujin's enemies, all at once, a very powerful leader and head. This leader was
a very influential chieftain named Yemuka. This Yemuka, it seems, was in love
with the daughter of Vang Khan, the Princess Wisulujine. He asked her in
marriage of her father. To precisely what state of forwardness the negotiations

36

had advanced does not appear, but, at any rate, when Temujin arrived, Wisulujine soon began to turn her thoughts toward him. He was undoubtedly younger, handsomer, and more accomplished than her old lover, and before long she gave her father to understand that she would much rather have him for her husband than Yemuka. It is true, Temujin had one or two wives already; but this made no difference, for it was the custom then, as, indeed, it is still, for the Asiatic princes and chieftains to take as many wives as their wealth and position would enable them to maintain. Yemuka was accordingly refused, and Wisulujine was given in marriage to Temujin.

Yemuka was, of course, dreadfully enraged. He vowed that he would be revenged. He immediately began to intrigue with all the discontented persons and parties in the kingdom, not only with those who were envious and jealous of Temujin, but also with all those who, for any reason, were disposed to put themselves in opposition to Vang Khan's government. Thus a formidable conspiracy was formed for the purpose of compassing Temujin's ruin.

The conspirators first tried the effect of private remonstrances with Vang Khan, in which they made all sorts of evil representations against Temujin, but to no effect. Temujin rallied about him so many old friends, and made so many new friends by his courage and energy, that his party at court proved stronger than that of his enemies, and, for a time, they seemed likely to fail entirely of their design.

At length the conspirators opened communication with the foreign enemies of Vang Khan, and formed a league with them to make war against and destroy both Vang Khan and Temujin together. The accounts of the progress of this league, and of the different nations and tribes which took part in it, is imperfect and confused; but at length, after various preliminary contests and manoeuvres, arrangements were made for assembling a large army with a view of invading Vang Khan's dominions and deciding the question by a battle. The different chieftains and khans whose troops were united to form this army bound themselves together by a solemn oath, according to the customs of those times, not to rest until both Vang Khan and Temujin should be destroyed.

The manner in which they took the oath was this: They brought out into an open space on the plain where they had assembled to take the oath, a horse, a wild ox, and a dog. At a given signal they fell upon these animals with their swords, and cut them all to pieces in the most furious manner. When they had finished, they stood together and called out aloud in the following words:

"Hear! O God! O heaven! O earth! the oath that we swear against Vang Khan and Temujin. If any one of us spares them when we have them in our power, or if we fail to keep the promise that we have made to destroy them, may we meet with the same fate that has befallen these beasts that we have now cut to pieces."

They uttered this imprecation in a very solemn manner, standing among the mangled and bloody remains of the beasts which lay strewed all about the ground.

These preparations had been made thus far very secretly; but tidings of what was going on came, before a great while, to Karakorom, Vang Khan's capital. Temujin was greatly excited when he heard the news. He immediately proposed that he should take his own troops, and join with them as many of Vang Khan's soldiers as could be conveniently spared, and go forth to meet the enemy. To this Vang Khan consented. Temujin took one half of Vang Khan's troops to join his own, leaving the other half to protect the capital, and so set forth on his expedition. He went off in the direction toward the frontier where he had understood the principal part of the hostile forces were assembling. After a long march, probably one of many days, he arrived there before the enemy was quite prepared for him. Then followed a series of manoeuvres and counter-manoeuvres, in which Temujin was all the time endeavoring to bring the rebels to battle, while they were doing all in their power to avoid it. Their object in this delay was to gain time for re-enforcements to come in, consisting of bodies of troops belonging to certain members of the league who had not yet arrived.

At length, when these manoeuvres were brought to an end, and the battle was about to be fought, Temujin and his whole army were one day greatly surprised to see his father-in-law, Vang Khan himself, coming into the camp at the head of a small and forlorn-looking band of followers, who had all the appearance of fugitives escaped from a battle. They looked anxious, way-worn, and exhausted, and the horses that they rode seemed wholly spent with fatigue and privation. On explanation, Temujin learned that, as soon as it was known that he had left the capital, and taken with him a large part of the army, a certain tribe of Vang Khan's enemies, living in another direction, had determined to seize the opportunity to invade his dominions, and had accordingly come suddenly in, with an immense horde, to attack the capital. Vang Khan had done all that he could to defend the city, but he had been overpowered. The greater part of his soldiers had been killed or wounded. The city had been taken and pillaged. His son, with those of the troops that had been able to save themselves, had escaped to the mountains. As to Vang Khan himself, he had thought it best to make his way, as soon as possible, to the camp of Temujin, where he had now arrived, after enduring great hardships and sufferings on the way.

Temujin was at first much amazed at hearing this story. He, however, bade his father-in-law not to be cast down or discouraged, and promised him full revenge, and a complete triumph over all his enemies at the coming battle. So he proceeded at once to complete his arrangements for the coming fight. He resigned to Vang Khan the command of the main body of the army, while he placed himself at the head of one of the wings, assigning the other to the chieftain next in rank in his army. In this order he went into battle.

The battle was a very obstinate and bloody one, but, in the end, Temujin's party was victorious. The troops opposed to him were defeated and driven off the field. The victory appeared to be due altogether to Temujin himself; for, after the struggle had continued a long time, and the result still appeared doubtful, the troops of Temujin's wing finally made a desperate charge, and forced their way with such fury into the midst of the forces of the enemy that nothing could withstand them. This encouraged and animated the other troops to such a degree that very soon the enemy were entirely routed and driven from off the field.

The effect of this victory was to raise the reputation of Temujin as a military commander higher than ever, and greatly to increase the confidence which Vang Khan was inclined to repose in him. The victory, too, seemed at first to have well-nigh broken up the party of the rebels. Still, the way was not yet open for Vang Khan to return and take possession of his throne and of his capital, for he learned that one of his brothers had assumed the government, and was reigning in Karakorom in his place. It would seem that this brother, whose name was Erkekara, had been one of the leaders of the party opposed to Temujin. It was natural that he should be so; for, being the brother of the king, he would, of course, occupy a very high position in the court, and would be one of the first to experience the ill effects produced by the coming in of any new favorite. He had accordingly joined in the plots that were formed against Temujin and Vang Khan. Indeed, he was considered, in some respects, as the head of their party, and when Vang Khan was driven away from his capital, this brother assumed the throne in his stead. The question was, how could he now be dispossessed and Vang Khan restored.

Temujin began immediately to form his plans for the accomplishment of this purpose. He concentrated his forces after the battle, and soon afterward opened negotiations with other tribes, who had before been uncertain which side to espouse, but were now assisted a great deal in coming to a decision by the victory which Temujin had obtained. In the mean time the rebels were not idle. They banded themselves together anew, and made great exertions to procure re-enforcements. Erkekara fortified himself as strongly as possible in Karakorom, and collected ample supplies of ammunition and military stores. It was not until the following year that the parties had completed their preparations and were prepared for the final struggle. Then, however, another great battle was fought, and again Temujin was victorious. Erkekara was killed or driven away in his turn. Karakorom was retaken, and Vang Khan entered it in triumph at the head of his troops, and was once more established on his throne.

Of course, the rank and influence of Temujin at his court was now higher than ever before. He was now about twenty-two or twenty-three years of age. He had already three wives, though it is not certain that all of them were with him at Vang Khan's court. He was extremely popular in the army, as young commanders of great courage and spirit almost always are. Vang Khan placed great reliance upon him, and lavished upon him all possible honors.

He does not seem, however, yet to have begun to form any plans for returning to his native land.

CHAPTER 7: RUPTURE WITH VANG KHAN
1182-1202

*Erkekara—State of the country—Wandering habits—Yemuka—Sankum—
Yemuka's intrigues with Sankum—Deceit—Temujin's situation—His military
expeditions—Popular commanders—Stories of Temujin's cruelty—Probably
fictions—Vang Khan's uneasiness—Temujin—Vang Khan's suspicions—A
reconciliation—Fresh suspicions—Plans laid—Treachery—Menglik—Menglik
gives Temujin warning—The double marriage—Plans frustrated—Temujin's
camp—Karasher—Vang Khan's plans—His plans betrayed by two slaves—How
the slaves overheard—A council called—Temujin plans a stratagem.*

Temujin remained at the court, or in the dominions of Vang Khan, for a great
many years. During the greater portion of this time he continued in the service of
Vang Khan, and on good terms with him, though, in the end, as we shall
presently see, their friendship was turned into a bitter enmity.

Erkekara, Vang Khan's brother, who had usurped his throne during the
rebellion, was killed, it was said, at the time when Vang Khan recovered his
throne. Several of the other rebel chieftains were also killed, but some of them
succeeded in saving themselves from utter ruin, and in gradually recovering their
former power over the hordes which they respectively commanded. It must be
remembered that the country was not divided at this time into regular territorial
states and kingdoms, but was rather one vast undivided region, occupied by
immense hordes, each of which was more or less stationary, it is true, in its own
district or range, but was nevertheless without any permanent settlement. The
various clans drifted slowly this way and that among the plains and mountains, as
the prospects of pasturage, the fortune of war, or the pressure of conterminous
hordes might incline them. In cases, too, where a number of hordes were united
under one general chieftain, as was the case with those over whom Vang Khan
claimed to have sway, the tie by which they were bound together was very
feeble, and the distinction between a state of submission and of rebellion, except
in case of actual war, was very slightly defined.

Yemuka, the chieftain who had been so exasperated against Temujin on
account of his being supplanted by him in the affections of the young princess,
Vang Khan's daughter, whom Temujin had married for his third wife, succeeded
in making his escape at the time when Vang Khan conquered his enemies and
recovered his throne. For a time he concealed himself, or at least kept out of

Vang Khan's reach, by dwelling with hordes whose range was at some distance from Karakorom. He soon, however, contrived to open secret negotiations with one of Vang Khan's sons, whose name was something that sounded like Sankum. Some authors, in attempting to represent his name in our letters, spelled it _Sunghim_.

Yemuka easily persuaded this young Sankum to take sides with him in the quarrel. It was natural that he should do so, for, being the son of Vang Khan, he was in some measure displaced from his own legitimate and proper position at his father's court by the great and constantly increasing influence which Temujin exercised.

"And besides," said Yemuka, in the secret representations which he made to Sankum, "this new-comer is not only interfering with and curtailing your proper influence and consideration now, but his design is by-and-by to circumvent and supplant you altogether. He is forming plans for making himself your father's heir, and so robbing you of your rightful inheritance."

Sankum listened very eagerly to these suggestions, and finally it was agreed between him and Yemuka that Sankum should exert his influence with his father to obtain permission for Yemuka to come back to court, and to be received again into his father's service, under pretense of having repented of his rebellion, and of being now disposed to return to his allegiance. Sankum did this, and, after a time, Vang Khan was persuaded to allow Yemuka to return.

Thus a sort of outward peace was made, but it was no real peace. Yemuka was as envious and jealous of Temujin as ever, and now, moreover, in addition to this envy and jealousy, he felt the stimulus of revenge. Things, however, seem to have gone on very quietly for a time, or at least without any open outbreak in the court. During this time Vang Khan was, as usual with such princes, frequently engaged in wars with the neighboring hordes. In these wars he relied a great deal on Temujin. Temujin was in command of a large body of troops, which consisted in part of his own guard, the troops that had come with him from his own country, and in part of other bands of men whom Vang Khan had placed under his orders, or who had joined him of their own accord. He was assisted in the command of this body by four subordinate generals or khans, whom he called his four intrepids. They were all very brave and skillful commanders. At the head of this troop Temujin was accustomed to scour the country, hunting out Vang Khan's enemies, or making long expeditions over distant plains or among the mountains, in the prosecution of Vang Khan's warlike projects, whether those of invasion and plunder, or of retaliation and vengeance.

Temujin was extremely popular with the soldiers who served under him. Soldiers always love a dashing, fearless, and energetic leader, who has the genius to devise brilliant schemes, and the spirit to execute them in a brilliant manner. They care very little how dangerous the situations are into which he may lead them. Those that get killed in performing the exploits which he undertakes can not speak to complain, and those who survive are only so much the better pleased that the dangers that they have been brought safely through were so desperate, and that the harvest of glory which they have thereby acquired is so great.

Temujin, though a great favorite with his own men, was, like almost all half-savage warriors of his class, utterly merciless, when he was angry, in his treatment of his enemies. It is said that after one of his battles, in which he had gained a complete victory over an immense horde of rebels and other foes, and had taken great numbers of them prisoners, he ordered fires to be built and seventy large caldrons of water to be put over them, and then, when the water was boiling hot, he caused the principal leaders of the vanquished army to be thrown in headlong and thus scalded to death. Then he marched at once into the country of the enemy, and there took all the women and children, and sent them off to be sold as slaves, and seized the cattle and other property which he found, and carried it off as plunder. In thus taking possession of the enemy's property and making it his own, and selling the poor captives into slavery, there was nothing remarkable. Such was the custom of the times. But the act of scalding his prisoners to death seems to denote or reveal in his character a vein of peculiar and atrocious cruelty. It is possible, however, that the story may not be true. It may have been invented by Yemuka and Sankum, or by some of his other enemies.

For Yemuka and Sankum, and others who were combined with them, were continually endeavoring to undermine Temujin's influence with Vang Khan, and thus deprive him of his power. But he was too strong for them. His great success in all his military undertakings kept him up in spite of all that his rivals could do to pull him down. As for Vang Khan himself, he was in part pleased with him and proud of him, and in part he feared him. He was very unwilling to be so dependent upon a subordinate chieftain, and yet he could not do without him. A king never desires that any one of his subjects should become too conspicuous or too great, and Vang Khan would have been very glad to have diminished, in some way, the power and prestige which Temujin had acquired, and which seemed to be increasing every day. He, however, found no means of effecting this in any quiet and peaceful manner. Temujin was at the head of his troops, generally away from Karakorom, where Vang Khan resided, and he was, in a great measure, independent. He raised his own recruits to keep the numbers of his army good, and it was always easy to subsist if there chanced to be any failure in the ordinary and regular supplies.

Besides, occasions were continually occurring in which Vang Khan wished for Temujin's aid, and could not dispense with it. At one time, while engaged in some important campaigns, far away among the mountains, Yemuka contrived to awaken so much distrust of Temujin in Vang Khan's mind, that Vang Khan secretly decamped in the night, and marched away to a distant place to save himself from a plot which Yemuka had told him that Temujin was contriving. Here, however, he was attacked by a large body of his enemies, and was reduced to such straits that he was obliged to send couriers off at once to Temujin to come with his intrepids and save him. Temujin came. He rescued Vang Khan from his danger, and drove his enemies away. Vang Khan was very grateful for this service, so that the two friends became entirely reconciled to each other, and were united more closely than ever, greatly to Yemuka's disappointment and chagrin. They made a new league of amity, and, to seal and confirm it, they agreed upon a double marriage between their two families. A son of Temujin was to be married to a daughter of Vang Khan, and a son of Vang Khan to a daughter of Temujin.

This new compact did not, however, last long. As soon as Vang Khan found that the danger from which Temujin had rescued him was passed, he began again to listen to the representations of Yemuka and Sankum, who still insisted that Temujin was a very dangerous man, and was by no means to be trusted. They said that he was ambitious and unprincipled, and that he was only waiting for a favorable opportunity to rebel himself against Vang Khan and depose him from his throne. They made a great many statements to the khan in confirmation of their opinion, some of which were true doubtless, but many were exaggerated, and others probably false. They, however, succeeded at last in making such an impression upon the khan's mind that he finally determined to take measures for putting Temujin out of the way.

Accordingly, on some pretext or other, he contrived to send Temujin away from Karakorom, his capital, for Temujin was so great a favorite with the royal guards and with all the garrison of the town, that he did not dare to undertake any thing openly against him there. Vang Khan also sent a messenger to Temujin's own country to persuade the chief persons there to join him in his plot. It will be recollected that, at the time that Temujin left his own country, when he was about fourteen years old, his mother had married a great chieftain there, named Menglik, and that this Menglik, in conjunction doubtless with Temujin's mother, had been made regent during his absence. Vang Khan now sent to Menglik to propose that he should unite with him to destroy Temujin.

"You have no interest," said Vang Khan in the message that he sent to Menglik, "in taking his part. It is true that you have married his mother, but, personally, he is nothing to you. And, if he is once out of the way, you will be acknowledged as the Grand Khan of the Monguls in your own right, whereas you now hold your place in subordination to him, and he may at any time return and set you aside altogether."

Vang Khan hoped by these arguments to induce Menglik to come and assist him in his plan of putting Temujin to death, or, at least, if Menglik would not assist him in perpetrating the deed, he thought that, by these arguments, he should induce him to be willing that it should be committed, so that he should himself have nothing to fear afterward from his resentment. But Menglik received the proposal in a very different way from what Vang Khan had expected. He said nothing, but he determined immediately to let Temujin know of the danger that he was in. He accordingly at once set out to go to Temujin's camp to inform him of Vang Khan's designs.

In the mean time, Vang Khan, having matured his plans, made an appointment for Temujin to meet him at a certain place designated for the purpose of consummating the double marriage between their children, which had been before agreed upon. Temujin, not suspecting any treachery, received and entertained the messenger in a very honorable manner, and said that he would come. After making the necessary preparations, he set out, in company with the messenger and with a grand retinue of his own attendants, to go to the place appointed. On his way he was met or overtaken by Menglik, who had come to warn him of his danger. As soon as Temujin had heard what his stepfather had to say, he made some excuse for postponing the journey, and, sending a civil answer to Vang Khan by the ambassador, he ordered him to go forward, and went back himself to his own camp.

This camp was at some distance from Karakorom. Vang Khan, as has already been stated, had sent Temujin away from the capital on account of his being so great a favorite that he was afraid of some tumult if he were to attempt any thing against him there. Temujin was, however, pretty strong in his camp. The troops that usually attended him were there, with the four intrepids as commanders of the four principal divisions of them. His old instructor and guardian, Karasher, was with him too. Karasher, it seems, had continued in Temujin's service up to this time, and was accustomed to accompany him in all his expeditions as his counselor and friend.

When Vang Khan learned, by the return of his messenger, that Temujin declined to come to the place of rendezvous which he had appointed, he concluded at once that he suspected treachery, and he immediately decided that he must now strike a decisive blow without any delay, otherwise Temujin would put himself more and more on his guard. He was not mistaken, it seems, however, in thinking how great a favorite Temujin was at Karakorom, for his secret design was betrayed to Temujin by two of his servants, who overheard him speak of it to one of his wives. Vang Khan's plan was to go out secretly to Temujin's camp at the head of an armed force superior to his, and there come upon him and his whole troop suddenly, by surprise, in the night, by which means, he thought, he should easily overpower the whole encampment, and either kill Temujin and his generals, or else make them prisoners. The two men who betrayed this plan were slaves, who were employed to take care of the horses of some person connected with Vang Khan's household, and to render various other services. Their names were Badu and Kishlik. It seems that these men were one day carrying some milk to Vang Khan's house or tent, and there they overheard a conversation between Vang Khan and his wife, by which they learned the particulars of the plan formed for Temujin's destruction. The expedition was to set out, they heard, on the following morning.

It is not at all surprising that they overheard this conversation, for not only the tents, but even the houses used by these Asiatic nations were built of very frail and thin materials, and the partitions were often made of canvas and felt, and other such substances as could have very little power to intercept sound.

The two slaves determined to proceed at once to Temujin's camp and warn him of his danger. So they stole away from their quarters at nightfall, and, after traveling diligently all night, in the morning they reached the camp and told Temujin what they had learned. Temujin was surprised; but he had been, in some measure, prepared for such intelligence by the communication which his stepfather had made him in respect to Vang Khan's treacherous designs a few days before. He immediately summoned Karasher and some of his other friends, in order to consult in respect to what it was best to do.

It was resolved to elude Vang Khan's design by means of a stratagem. He was to come upon them, according to the account of the slaves, that night. The preparations for receiving him were consequently to be made at once. The plan was for Temujin and all his troops to withdraw from the camp and conceal themselves in a place of ambuscade near by. They were to leave a number of men behind, who, when night came on, were to set the lights and replenish the fires, and put everything in such a condition as to make it appear that the troops were all there. Their expectation was that, when Vang Khan should arrive, he would make his assault according to his original design, and then, while his forces were in the midst of the confusion incident to such an onset, Temujin was to come forth from his ambuscade and fall upon them. In this way he hoped to conquer them and put them to flight, although he had every reason to suppose that the force which Vang Khan would bring out against him would be considerably stronger in numbers than his own.

CHAPTER 8: PROGRESS OF THE QUARREL
1202

The ambuscade—The wood and the brook—The guard left behind—Arrival of Vang Khan's army—False hopes—Assault upon the vacant camp—Advance of the assailants—The ambuscade—Temujin's victory—Preparations for open war—Temujin makes alliances—Turkili—Solemn league and covenant—Bitter water—Recollection of the ceremony—Temujin's strength—His letter to Vang Khan—Effect of the letter—Sankum's anger—Great accessions to Temujin's army—Mongolistan—Final attempt at negotiation—Sankum's answer—Skirmishes.

Temujin's stratagem succeeded admirably. As soon as he had decided upon it he began to put it into execution. He caused everything of value to be taken out of his tent and carried away to a place of safety. He sent away the women and children, too, to the same place. He then marshaled all his men, excepting the small guard that he was going to leave behind until evening, and led them off to the ambuscade which he had chosen for them. The place was about two leagues distant from his camp. Temujin concealed himself here in a narrow dell among the mountains, not far from the road where Vang Khan would have to pass along. The dell was narrow, and was protected by precipitous rocks on each side. There was a wood at the entrance to it also, which concealed those that were hidden in it from view, and a brook which flowed by near the entrance, so that, in going in or coming out, it was necessary to ford the brook.

Temujin, on arriving at the spot, went with all his troops into the dell, and concealed himself there.

In the mean time, the guard that had been left behind in the camp had been instructed to kindle up the camp-fires as soon as the evening came on, according to the usual custom, and to set lights in the tents, so as to give the camp the appearance, when seen from a little distance in the night, of being occupied, as usual, by the army. They were to wait, and watch the fires and lights until they perceived signs of the approach of the enemy to attack the camp, when they were secretly to retire on the farther side, and so make their escape.

These preparations, and the march of Temujin's troops to the place of ambuscade, occupied almost the whole of the day, and it was near evening before the last of the troops had entered the dell.

They had scarce accomplished this manoeuvre before Vang Khan's army arrived. Vang Khan himself was not with them. He had intrusted the expedition to the command of Sankum and Yemuka. Indeed, it is probable that they were the real originators and contrivers of it, and that Vang Khan had only been induced to give his consent to it—and that perhaps reluctantly—by their persuasions. Sankum and Yemuka advanced cautiously at the head of their columns, and when they saw the illumination of the camp produced by the lights and the camp-fires, they thought at once that all was right, and that their old enemy and rival was now, at last, within their reach and at their mercy.

They brought up the men as near to the camp as they could come without being observed, and then, drawing their bows and making their arrows ready, they advanced furiously to the onset, and discharged an immense shower of arrows in among the tents. They expected to see thousands of men come rushing out from the tents, or starting up from the ground at this sudden assault, but, to their utter astonishment, all was as silent and motionless after the falling of the arrows as before. They then discharged more arrows, and, finding that they could not awaken any signs of life, they began to advance cautiously and enter the camp. They found, of course, that it had been entirely evacuated. They then rode round and round the inclosure, examining the ground with flambeaux and torches to find the tracks which Temujin's army had made in going away. The tracks were soon discovered. Those who first saw them immediately set off in pursuit of the fugitives, as they supposed them, shouting, at the same time, for the rest to follow. Some did follow immediately. Others, who had strayed away to greater or less distances on either side of the camp in search of the tracks, fell in by degrees as they received the order, while others still remained among the tents, where they were to be seen riding to and fro, endeavoring to make discoveries, or gathering together in groups to express to one another their astonishment, or to inquire what was next to be done. They, however, all gradually fell into the ranks of those who were following the track which had been found, and the whole body went on as fast as they could go, and in great confusion. They all supposed that Temujin and his troops were making a precipitate retreat, and were expecting every moment to come up to him in his rear, in which case he would be taken at great disadvantage, and would be easily overwhelmed.

Instead of this, Temujin was just coming forward from his hiding-place, with his squadrons all in perfect order, and advancing in a firm, steady, and compact column, all being ready at the word of command to charge in good order, but with terrible impetuosity, upon the advancing enemy. In this way the two armies came together. The shock of the encounter was terrific. Temujin, as might have been expected, was completely victorious. The confused masses of Vang Khan's army were overborne, thrown into dreadful confusion, and trampled underfoot. Great numbers were killed. Those that escaped being killed at once turned and fled. Sankum was wounded in the face by an arrow, but he still was able to keep his seat upon his horse, and so galloped away. Those that succeeded in saving themselves got back as soon as they could into the road by which they came, and so made their way, in detached and open parties, home to Karakorom.

Of course, after this, Vang Khan could no longer dissimulate his hostility to Temujin, and both parties prepared for open war.

The different historians through whom we derive our information in respect to the life and adventures of Genghis Khan have related the transactions which occurred after this open outbreak between Temujin and Vang Khan somewhat differently. Combining their accounts, we learn that both parties, after the battle, opened negotiations with such neighboring tribes as they supposed likely to take sides in the conflict, each endeavoring to gain as many adherents as possible to his own cause. Temujin obtained the alliance and co-operation of a great number of Tartar princes who ruled over hordes that dwelt in that part of the country, or among the mountains around. Some of these chieftains were his relatives. Others were induced to join him by being convinced that he would, in the end, prove to be stronger than Vang Khan, and being, in some sense, politicians as well as warriors, they wished to be sure of coming out at the close of the contest on the victorious side.

There was a certain khan, named Turkili, who was a relative of Temujin, and who commanded a very powerful tribe. On approaching the confines of his territory, Temujin, not being certain of Turkili's disposition toward him, sent forward an ambassador to announce his approach, and to ask if Turkili still retained the friendship which had long subsisted between them. Turkili might, perhaps, have hesitated which side to join, but the presence of Temujin with his whole troop upon his frontier seems to have determined him, so he sent a favorable answer, and at once espoused Temujin's cause.

Many other chieftains joined Temujin in much the same way, and thus the forces under his command were constantly increased. At length, in his progress across the country, he came with his troop of followers to a place where there was a stream of salt or bitter water which was unfit to drink. Temujin encamped on the shores of this stream, and performed a grand ceremony, in which he himself and his allies banded themselves together in the most solemn manner. In the course of the ceremony a horse was sacrificed on the shores of the stream. Temujin also took up some of the water from the brook and drank it, invoking heaven, at the same time, to witness a solemn vow which he made, that, as long as he lived, he would share with his officers and soldiers the bitter as well as the sweet, and imprecating curses upon himself if he should ever violate his oath. All his allies and officers did the same after him.

DRINKING FROM THE BITTER WATERS.

This ceremony was long remembered in the army, all those who had been present and had taken part in it cherishing the recollection of it with pride and pleasure; and long afterward, when Temujin had attained to the height of his power and glory, his generals considered their having been present at this first solemn league and covenant as conferring upon them a sort of title of nobility, by which they and their descendants were to be distinguished forever above all those whose adhesion to the cause of the conqueror dated from a later time.

By this time Temujin began to feel quite strong. He moved on with his army till he came to the borders of a lake which was not a great way from Vang Khan's dominions. Here he encamped, and, before proceeding any farther, he determined to try the effect, upon the mind of Vang Khan, of a letter of expostulation and remonstrance; so he wrote to him, substantially, as follows:

"A great many years ago, in the time of my father, when you were driven from your throne by your enemies, my father came to your aid, defeated your enemies, and restored you.

"At a later time, after I had come into your dominions, your brother conspired against you with the Markats and the Naymans. I defeated them,

51

and helped you to recover your   power. When you were reduced to great distress, I shared   with you my flocks and everything that I had.

"At another time, when you were in circumstances of great   danger and distress, you sent to me to ask that my four   intrepids might go and rescue you. I sent them according to   your request, and they delivered you from a most imminent   danger. They helped you to conquer your enemies, and to recover an immense booty from them.

"In many other instances, when the khans have combined   against you, I have given you most effectual aid in subduing   them.

"How is it, then, after receiving all these benefits from me   for a period of so many years, that you form plans to   destroy me in so base and treacherous a manner?"

This letter seems to have produced some impression upon Vang Khan's mind; but he was now, it seems, so much under the influence of Sankum and Yemuka that he could decide nothing for himself. He sent the letter to Sankum to ask him what answer should be returned. But Sankum, in addition to his former feelings of envy and jealousy against Temujin, was now irritated and angry in consequence of the wound that he had received, and determined to have his revenge. He would not hear of any accommodation.

In the mean time, the khans of all the Tartar and Mongul tribes that lived in the countries bordering on Vang Khan's dominions, hearing of the rupture between Vang Khan and Temujin, and aware of the great struggle for the mastery between these two potentates that was about to take place, became more and more interested in the quarrel. Temujin was very active in opening negotiations with them, and in endeavoring to induce them to take his side. He was a comparatively young and rising man, while Vang Khan was becoming advanced in years, and was now almost wholly under the influence of Sankum and Yemuka. Temujin, moreover, had already acquired great fame and great popularity as a commander, and his reputation was increasing every day, while Vang Khan's glory was evidently on the wane. A great number of the khans were, of course, predisposed to take Temujin's side. Others he compelled to join him by force, and others he persuaded by promising to release them from the exactions and the tyranny which Vang Khan had exercised over them, and declaring that he was a messenger especially sent from heaven to accomplish their deliverance. Those Asiatic tribes were always ready to believe in military messengers sent from heaven to make conquests for their benefit.

Among other nations who joined Temujin at this time were the people of his own country of Mongolistan Proper. He was received very joyfully by his stepfather, who was in command there, and by all his former subjects, and they all promised to sustain him in the coming war.

After a time, when Temujin had by these and similar means greatly increased the number of his adherents, and proportionately strengthened his position, he sent an ambassador again to Vang Khan to propose some accommodation. Vang Khan called a council to consider the proposal. But Sankum and Yemuka persisted in refusing to allow any accommodation to be made. They declared that they would not listen to proposals of peace on any other condition than that of the absolute surrender of Temujin, and of all who were confederate with him, to Vang Khan as their lawful sovereign. Sankum himself delivered the message to the ambassador.

"Tell the rebel Monguls," said he, "that they are to expect no peace but by submitting absolutely to the khan's will; and as for Temujin, I will never see him again till I come to him sword in hand to kill him."

Immediately after this Sankum and Yemuka sent off some small plundering expeditions into the Mongul country, but they were driven back by Temujin's troops without effecting their purpose. The result of these skirmishes was, however, greatly to exasperate both parties, and to lead them to prepare in earnest for open war.

CHAPTER 9: THE DEATH OF VANG KHAN
1202

A council called—Mankerule—Debates—Temujin made general-in-chief—He distributes rewards—Reward of the two slaves—His reasons—Organization of the army—Mode of attack—The two armies—The baggage—Meeting of the two armies—The battle—Vang Khan defeated—His flight—His relations with the Naymans—Debates among the Naymans—Tayian—Plan of the chieftains—Vang Khan beheaded—Tayian's deceit—Disposal made of his head—Sankum slain.

A grand council was now called of all the confederates who were leagued with Temujin, at a place called Mankerule, to make arrangements for a vigorous prosecution of the war. At this council were convened all the chieftains and khans that had been induced to declare against Vang Khan. Each one came attended by a considerable body of troops as his escort, and a grand deliberation was held. Some were in favor of trying once more to come to some terms of accommodation with Vang Khan, but Temujin convinced them that there was nothing to be hoped for except on condition of absolute submission, and that, in that case, Vang Khan would never be content until he had effected the utter ruin of everyone who had been engaged in the rebellion. So it was, at last, decided that every man should return to his own tribe, and there raise as large a force as he could, with a view to carrying on the war with the utmost vigor.

Temujin was formally appointed general-in-chief of the army to be raised. There was a sort of truncheon or ornamented club, called the topaz, which it was customary on such occasions to bestow, with great solemnity, on the general thus chosen, as his badge of command. The topaz was, in this instance, conferred upon Temujin with all the usual ceremonies. He accepted it on the express condition that every man would punctually and implicitly obey all his orders, and that he should have absolute power to punish anyone who should disobey him in the way that he judged best, and that they should submit without question to all his decisions. To these conditions they all solemnly agreed.

Being thus regularly placed in command, Temujin began by giving places of honor and authority to those who left Vang Khan's service to follow him. He took this occasion to remember and reward the two slaves who had come to him in the night at his camp, some time before, to give him warning of the design of Sankum and Yemuka to come and surprise him there. He gave the slaves their freedom, and made provision for their maintenance as long as they should live.

He also put them on the list of _exempts_. The exempts were a class of persons upon whom, as a reward for great public services, were conferred certain exclusive rights and privileges. They had no taxes to pay. In case of plunder taken from the enemy, they received their full share without any deduction, while all the others were obliged to contribute a portion of their shares for the khan. The exempts, too, were allowed various other privileges. They had the right to go into the presence of the khan at any time, without waiting, as others were obliged to do, till they obtained permission, and, what was more singular still, they were entitled to _nine_ pardons for any offenses that they might commit, so that it was only when they had committed ten misdemeanors or crimes that they were in danger of punishment The privileges which Temujin thus bestowed upon the slaves were to be continued to their descendants to the seventh generation.

Temujin rewarded the slaves in this bountiful manner, partly, no doubt, out of sincere gratitude to them for having been the means, probably, of saving him and his army from destruction, and partly for effect, in order to impress upon his followers a strong conviction that any great services rendered to him or to his cause were certain to be well rewarded.

Temujin now found himself at the head of a very large body of men, and his first care was to establish a settled system of discipline among them, so that they could act with regularity and order when coming into battle. He divided his army into three separate bodies. The centre was composed of his own guards, and was commanded by himself. The wings were formed of the squadrons of his confederates and allies. His plan in coming into battle was to send forward the two wings, retaining the centre as a reserve, and hold them prepared to rush in with irresistible power whenever the time should arrive at which their coming would produce the greatest effect.

When everything was thus arranged, Temujin set his army in motion, and began to advance toward the country of Vang Khan. The squadrons which composed his immense horde were so numerous that they covered all the plain.

In the mean time Vang Khan had not been idle. He, or rather Sankum and Yemuka, acting in his name, had assembled a great army, and he had set out on his march from Karakorom to meet his enemy. His forces, however, though more numerous, were by no means so well disciplined and arranged as those of Temujin. They were greatly encumbered, too, with baggage, the army being followed in its march by endless trains of wagons conveying provisions, arms, and military stores of all kinds. Its progress was, therefore, necessarily slow, for the troops of horsemen were obliged to regulate their speed by the movement of the wagons, which, on account of the heavy burdens that they contained, and the want of finished roads, was necessarily slow.

The two armies met upon a plain between two rivers, and a most desperate and bloody battle ensued. Karasher, Temujin's former tutor, led one of the divisions of Temujin's army, and was opposed by Yemuka, who headed the wing of Vang Khan's army which confronted his division. The other wings attacked each other, too, in the most furious manner, and for three hours it was doubtful which party would be successful. At length Temujin, who had all this time remained in the background with his reserve, saw that the favorable moment had arrived for him to intervene, and he gave the order for his guards to charge, which they did with such impetuosity as to carry all before them. One after another of Vang Khan's squadrons was overpowered, thrown into confusion, and driven from the field. It was not long before Vang Khan saw that all was lost. He gave up the contest and fled. A small troop of horsemen, consisting of his immediate attendants and guards, went with him. At first the fugitives took the road toward Karakorom. They were, however, so hotly pursued that they were obliged to turn off in another direction, and, finally, Vang Khan resolved to fly from his own country altogether, and appeal for protection to a certain chieftain, named Tayian Khan, who ruled over a great horde called the Naymans, one of the most powerful tribes in the country of Karakatay. This Tayian was the father of Temujin's first wife, the young princess to whom he was married during the lifetime of his father, when he was only about fourteen years old.

It was thought strange that Vang Khan should thus seek refuge among the Naymans, for he had not, for some time past, been on friendly terms either with Tayian, the khan, or with the tribe. There were, in particular, a considerable number of the subordinate chieftains who cherished a deep-seated resentment against him for injuries which he had inflicted upon them and upon their country in former wars. But all these Tartar tribes entertained very high ideas of the obligations of hospitality, and Vang Khan thought that when the Naymans saw him coming among them, a fugitive and in distress, they would lay aside their animosity, and give him a kind reception.

Indeed, Tayian himself, on whom, as the head of the tribe, the chief discredit would attach of any evil befalling a visitor and a guest who had come in his distress to seek hospitality, was inclined, at first, to receive his enemy kindly, and to offer him a refuge. He debated the matter with the other chieftains after Vang Khan had entered his dominions and was approaching his camp; but they were extremely unwilling that any mercy should be shown to their fallen enemy. They represented to Tayian how great an enemy he had always been to them. They exaggerated the injuries which he had done them, and represented them in their worst light. They said, moreover, that, by harboring Vang Khan, they should only involve themselves in a war with Temujin, who would undoubtedly follow his enemy into their country, and would greatly resent any attempt on their part to protect him.

These considerations had great effect on the mind of Tayian, but still he could not bring himself to give his formal consent to any act of hostility against Vang Khan. So the other chieftains held a council among themselves to consider what they should do. They resolved to take upon themselves the responsibility of slaying Vang Khan.

"We can not induce Tayian openly to authorize it," they said, "but he secretly desires it, and he will be glad when it is done."

Tayian knew very well what course things were taking, though he pretended not to know, and so allowed the other chiefs to go on in their own way.

They accordingly fitted out a troop, and two of the chieftains—the two who felt the most bitter and determined hatred against Vang Khan—placing themselves at the head of it, set off to intercept him. He had lingered on the way, it seems, after entering the Nayman territory, in order to learn, before he advanced too far, what reception he was likely to meet with. The troop of Naymans came suddenly upon him in his encampment, slew all his attendants, and, seizing Vang Khan, they cut off his head. They left the body where it lay, and carried off the head to show it to Tayian.

Tayian was secretly pleased, and he could not quite conceal the gratification which the death of his old enemy afforded him. He even addressed the head in words of scorn and spite, which revealed the exultation that he felt at the downfall of his rival. Then, however, checking himself, he blamed the chieftains for killing him.

"Considering his venerable age," said he, "and his past greatness and renown as a prince and commander, you would have done much better to have acted as his guards than as his executioners."

Tayian ordered the head to be treated with the utmost respect. After properly preparing it, by some process of drying and preserving, he caused it to be inclosed in a case of silver, and set in a place of honor.

While the preparations for this sort of entombment were making, the head was an object of a very solemn and mysterious interest for all the horde. They said that the tongue thrust itself several times out of the mouth, and the soothsayers, who watched the changes with great attention, drew from them important presages in respect to the coming events of the war. These presages were strongly in favor of the increasing prosperity and power of Temujin.

Sankum, the son of Vang Khan, was killed in the battle, but Yemuka escaped.

CHAPTER 10: THE DEATH OF YEMUKA
1202-1203

The victory complete—Exaggeration—The plunder—Great accession—The khans submit—Sankum and Yemuka—Hakembu and his daughter—Hakembu's fears—Temujin's gratitude—His reply—Yemuka makes his escape—Arrives in Tayian's dominions—Tayian's conversations with Yemuka—Yemuka's representations of Temujin's character—Plots formed—Alakus—The plots revealed to Temujin—He is deceived—The young Prince Jughi—Council of war—Yemuka and Tayian—Temujin crosses the frontier—His advance—Preparations for battle—Kushluk and Jughi—Great battle—Temujin again victorious—Tayian killed—Yemuka is beheaded.

In the mean time, while these events had been occurring in the country of the Naymans, whither Vang Khan had fled, Temujin was carrying all before him in the country of Vang Khan. His victory in the battle was complete; and it must have been a very great battle, if any reliance is to be placed on the accounts given of the number slain, which it was said amounted to forty thousand. These numbers are, however, greatly exaggerated. And then, besides, the number slain in such barbarian conflicts was always much greater, in proportion to the numbers engaged, than it is in the better-regulated warfare of civilized nations in modern times.

At all events, Temujin gained a very grand and decisive victory. He took a great many prisoners and a great deal of plunder. All those trains of wagons fell into his hands, and the contents of many of them were extremely valuable. He took also a great number of horses. Most of these were horses that had belonged to the men who were killed or who had been made prisoners. All the best troops that remained of Vang Khan's army after the battle also went over to his side. They considered that Vang Khan's power was now entirely overthrown, and that thenceforth Temujin would be the acknowledged ruler of the whole country. They were accordingly ready at once to transfer their allegiance to him.

Very soon Temujin received the news of Vang Khan's death from his father-in-law Tayian, and then proceeded with more vigor than before to take possession of all his dominions. The khans who had formerly served under Vang Khan sent in their adhesion to him one after another. They not only knew that all farther resistance would be useless, but they were, in fact, well pleased to transfer their allegiance to their old friend and favorite. Temujin made a sort of triumphal march through the country, being received every where with rejoicings and acclamations of welcome. His old enemies, Sankum and Yemuka, had disappeared. Yemuka, who had been, after all, the leading spirit in the opposition to Temujin, still held a body of armed men together, consisting of all the troops that he had been able to rally after the battle, but it was not known exactly where he had gone.

The other relatives and friends of Vang Khan went over to Temujin's side without any delay. Indeed, they vied with each other to see who should most recommend themselves to his favor. A brother of Vang Khan, who was an influential and powerful chieftain, came among the rest to tender his services, and, by way of a present to conciliate Temujin's good will, he brought him his daughter, whom he offered to Temujin as an addition to the number of his wives.

Temujin received the brother very kindly. He accepted the present which he brought him of his daughter, but, as he had already plenty of wives, and as one of his principal officers, the captain of his guards, seemed to take a special fancy to her, he very generously, as was thought, passed over the young lady to him. Of course, the young lady herself had nothing to say in the case. She was obliged to acquiesce submissively in any arrangement which her father and the other khans thought proper to make in respect to the disposal of her.

The name of the prince her father was Hakembu. He came into Temujin's camp with many misgivings, fearing that, as he was a brother of Vang Khan, Temujin might feel a special resentment against him, and, perhaps, refuse to accept his submission and his proffered presents. When, therefore, he found how kindly he was received, his mind was greatly relieved, and he asked Temujin to appoint him to some command in his army.

Temujin replied that he would do it with great pleasure, and the more readily because it was the brother of Vang Khan who asked it. "Indeed," said he to Hakembu, "I owe you all the kind treatment in my power for your brother's sake, in return for the succor and protection for which I was indebted to him, in my misfortunes, in former times, when he received me, a fugitive and an exile, at his court, and bestowed upon me so many favors. I have never forgotten, and never shall forget, the great obligations I am under to him; and although in later years he turned against me, still I have never blamed either him or his son Sankum for this, but have constantly attributed it to the false representations and evil influence of Yemuka, who has always been my implacable enemy. I do not, therefore, feel any resentment against Vang Khan for having thus turned against me, nor do I any the less respect his memory on that account; and I am very glad that an opportunity now occurs for me to make, through you, his brother, some small acknowledgment of the debt of gratitude which I owe him."

So Temujin gave Hakembu an honorable post in his army, and treated him in all respects with great consideration. If he acted usually in this generous manner, it is not at all surprising that he acquired that boundless influence over the minds of his followers which aided him so essentially in attaining his subsequent greatness and renown.

In the mean time, although Sankum was killed, Yemuka had succeeded in making his escape, and, after meeting with various adventures, he finally reached the country of Tayian. He led with him there all that portion of Vang Khan's army that had saved themselves from being killed or made prisoners, and also a great number of officers. These broken troops Yemuka had reorganized, as well as he could, by collecting the scattered remnants and rearranging the broken squadrons, and in this manner, accompanied by such of the sick and wounded as were able to ride, had arrived in Tayian's dominions. He was known to be a general of great abilities, and he was very favorably received in Tayian's court. Indeed, Tayian, having heard rumors of the rapid manner in which Temujin was extending his conquests and his power, began to be somewhat jealous of him, and to think that it was time for him to take measures to prevent this aggrandizement of his son-in-law from going too far.

Of course, Tayian held a great many conversations with Yemuka in respect to Temujin's character and schemes. These Yemuka took care to represent in the most unfavorable light, in order to increase as much as possible Tayian's feelings of suspicion and jealousy. He represented Temujin as a very ambitious man, full of schemes for his own aggrandizement, and without any sentiments of gratitude or of honor to restrain him in the execution of them. He threw wholly upon him the responsibility of the war with Vang Khan. It grew, he said, out of plots which Temujin had formed to destroy both Vang Khan and his son, notwithstanding the great obligations he had been under to them for their kindness to him in his misfortunes. Yemuka urged Tayian also to arouse himself, before it was too late, to guard himself from the danger.

"He is your son, it is true," said he, "and he professes to be your friend, but he is so treacherous and unprincipled that you can place no reliance upon him whatever, and, notwithstanding all your past kindness to him, and the tie of relationship which ought to bind him to you, he will as readily form plans to compass your destruction as he would that of any other man the moment he imagines that you stand in the way of the accomplishment of his ambitious schemes."

These representations, acting upon Tayian's natural apprehensions and fears, produced a very sensible effect, and at length Tayian was induced to take some measures for defending himself from the threatened danger. So he opened negotiations with the khans of various tribes which he thought likely to join him, and soon formed quite a powerful league of the enemies of Temujin, and of all who were willing to join in an attempt to restrict his power.

These steps were all taken with great secrecy, for Yemuka and Tayian were very desirous that Temujin should know nothing of the league which they were forming against him until their arrangements were fully matured, and they were ready for action. They did not, however, succeed in keeping the secret as long as they intended. They were generally careful not to propose to any khan or chieftain to join them in their league until they had first fully ascertained that he was favorable to the object of it. But, growing less cautious as they went on, they at last made a mistake. Tayian sent proposals to a certain prince or khan, named Alakus, inviting him to join the league. These proposals were contained in a letter which was sent by a special messenger. The letter specified all the particulars of the league, with a statement of the plans which the allies were intending to pursue, and an enumeration of the principal khans or tribes that were already engaged.

Now it happened that this Alakus, who reigned over a nation of numerous and powerful tribes on the confines of China, was, for some reason or other, inclined to take Temujin's side in the quarrel. So he detained the messenger who brought the letter as a prisoner, and sent the letter itself, containing all the particulars of the conspiracy, at once to Temujin. Temujin was greatly surprised at receiving the intelligence, for, up to that moment, he had considered his father-in-law Tayian as one of his best and most trustworthy friends. He immediately called a grand council of war to consider what was to be done.

Temujin had a son named Jughi, who had now grown up to be a young man. Jughi's father thought it was now time for his son to begin to take his place and act his part among the other princes and chieftains of his court, and he accordingly gave him a seat at this council, and thus publicly recognized him, for the first time, as one of the chief personages of the state.

The council, after hearing a statement of the case in respect to the league which Tayian and the others were forming, were strongly inclined to combine their forces and march at once to attack the enemy before their plans should be more fully matured. But there was a difficulty in respect to horses. The horses of the different hordes that belonged to Temujin's army had become so much exhausted by the long marches and other fatigues that they had undergone in the late campaigns, that they would not be in a fit condition to commence a new expedition until they had had some time to rest and recruit. But a certain khan, named Bulay, an uncle of Temujin's, at once removed this objection by offering to furnish a full supply of fresh horses for the whole army from his own herds.

61

This circumstance shows on what an immense scale the pastoral occupations of the great Asiatic chieftains were conducted in those days.

Temujin accepted this offer on the part of his uncle, and preparations were immediately made for the marching of the expedition. As soon as the news of these preparations reached Yemuka, he urged Tayian to assemble the allied troops immediately, and go out to meet Temujin and his army before they should cross the frontier.

"It is better," said he, addressing Tayian, "that you should meet and fight him on his own ground, rather than to wait until he has crossed the frontier and commenced his ravages in yours."

"No," said Tayian, in reply, "it is better to wait. The farther he advances on his march, the more his horses and his men will be spent with fatigue, the scantier will be their supplies, and the more difficult will he find it to effect his retreat after we shall have gained a victory over him in battle."

So Tayian, though he began to assemble his forces, did not advance; and when Temujin, at the head of his host, reached the Nayman frontier—for the country over which Tayian reigned was called the country of the Naymans—he was surprised to find no enemy there to defend it. He was the more surprised at this from the circumstance that the frontier, being formed by a river, might have been very easily defended. But when he arrived at the bank of the river the way was clear. He immediately crossed the stream with all his forces, and then marched on into the Nayman territory.

Temujin took good care, as he advanced, to guard against the danger into which Tayian had predicted that he would fall—that of exhausting the strength of his men and of his animals, and also his stores of food. He took good care to provide and to take with him abundant supplies, and also to advance so carefully and by such easy stages as to keep both the men and the horses fresh and in full strength all the way. In this order and condition he at last arrived at the spot where Tayian had formed his camp and assembled his armies.

Both sides immediately marshaled their troops in order of battle. Yemuka was chief in command on Tayian's side. He was assisted by a young prince, the son of Tayian, whose name was Kushluk. On the other hand, Jughi, the young son of Temujin, who had been brought forward at the council, was appointed to a very prominent position on his father's side. Indeed, these two young princes, who were animated by an intense feeling of rivalry and emulation toward each other, were appointed to lead the van on their respective sides in commencing the battle; Jughi advancing first to the attack, and being met by Kushluk, to whom was committed the charge of repelling him. The two princes fought throughout the battle with the utmost bravery, and both of them acquired great renown.

The battle was commenced early in the morning and continued all day. In the end, Temujin was completely victorious. Tayian was mortally wounded early in the day. He was immediately taken off the field, and every possible effort was made to save his life, but he soon ceased to breathe. His son, the Prince Kushluk, fought valiantly during the whole day, but toward night, finding that all was lost, he fled, taking with him as many of the troops as he could succeed in getting together in the confusion, and at the head of this band made the best of his way into the dominions of one of his uncles, his father's brother, where he hoped to find a temporary shelter until he should have time to determine what was to be done.

As for Yemuka, after fighting with desperate fury all day, he was at last, toward night, surrounded and overpowered, and so made prisoner. Temujin ordered his head to be cut off immediately after the battle was over. He considered him, not as an honorable and open foe, but rather as a rebel and traitor, and, consequently, undeserving of any mercy.

CHAPTER 11: ESTABLISHMENT OF THE EMPIRE
1203

Plans for the formation of a government—His court at Karakorom—Ambassadors—Temujin forms a constitution—Election of khans—Division of the country—Organization of the army—Arms and ammunition—Hunting—Slaves—Polygamy and slavery—Concubines—Posthumous marriages—Punishment for theft—Religion—Freedom of choice—Assembly of the khans—Dilon Ildak—Their encampment—Tents and herds of cattle—Temujin's address—Temujin is elected grand khan—He is enthroned and honored—The old prophet Kokza—Probably insane—His predictions—The title Genghis Khan—Homage of the khans—Inaugural address—Rejoicings—Departure of the khans.

There was now a vast extent of country, comprising a very large portion of the interior of the Asiatic Continent, and, indeed, an immense number of wealthy, powerful hordes, under Temujin's dominion, and he at once resolved to consolidate his dominion by organizing a regular imperial government over the whole. There were a few more battles to be fought in order to subdue certain khans who still resisted, and some cities to be taken. But these victories were soon obtained, and, in a very short time after the great battle with Tayian, Temujin found himself the undisputed master of what to him was almost the whole known world. All open opposition to his rule had wholly disappeared, and nothing now remained for him to do but to perfect the organization of his army, to enact his code of laws, to determine upon his capital, and to inaugurate generally a system of civil government such as is required for the management of the internal affairs of a great empire.

Temujin determined upon making Karakorom his capital. He accordingly proceeded to that city at the head of his troops, and entered it in great state. Here he established a very brilliant court, and during all the following winter, while he was occupied with the preliminary arrangements for the organization and consolidation of his empire, there came to him there a continual succession of ambassadors from the various nations and tribes of Central Asia to congratulate him on his victories, and to offer the allegiance or the alliance of the khans which they respectively represented. These ambassadors all came attended by troops of horsemen splendidly dressed and fully armed, and the gayety and magnificence of the scenes which were witnessed in Karakorom during the winter surpassed all that had ever been seen there before.

In the mean time, while the attention of the masses of the people was occupied and amused by these parades, Temujin was revolving in his mind the form of constitution which he should establish for his empire, and the system of laws by which his people should be governed. He conferred privately with some of his ablest counselors on this subject, and caused a system of government and a code of laws to be drawn up by secretaries. The details of these proposed enactments were discussed in the privy council, and, when the whole had been well digested and matured, Temujin, early in the spring, sent out a summons, calling upon all the great princes and khans throughout his dominions to assemble at an appointed day, in order that he might lay his proposed system before them.

Temujin determined to make his government a sort of elective monarchy. The grand khan was to be chosen by the votes of all the other khans, who were to be assembled in a general convocation for this purpose whenever a new khan was to be installed. Any person who should cause himself to be proclaimed grand khan, or who should in any other way attempt to assume the supreme authority without having been duly elected by the other khans, was to suffer death.

The country was divided into provinces, over each of which a subordinate khan ruled as governor. These governors were, however, to be strictly responsible to the grand khan. Whenever summoned by the grand khan they were required to repair at once to the capital, there to render an account of their administration, and to answer any charges which had been made against them. Whenever any serious case of disobedience or maladministration was proved against them they were to suffer death.

Temujin remodeled and reorganized the army on the same or similar principles. The men were divided into companies of about one hundred men each, and every ten of these companies was formed into a regiment, which, of course, contained about a thousand men. The regiments were formed into larger bodies of about ten thousand each. Officers were appointed, of all the various necessary grades, to command these troops, and arrangements were made for having supplies of arms and ammunition provided and stored in magazines under the care of the officers, ready to be distributed to the men whenever they should require.

Temujin also made provision for the building of cities and palaces, the making of roads, and the construction of fortifications, by ordaining that all the people should work one day in every week on these public works whenever required.

Although the country over which this new government was to be established was now at peace, Temujin was very desirous that the people should not lose the martial spirit which had thus far characterized them. He made laws to encourage and regulate hunting, especially the hunting of wild beasts among the mountains; and subsequently he organized many hunting excursions himself, in connection with the lords of his court and the other great chieftains, in order to awaken an interest in the dangers and excitements of the chase among all the khans. He also often employed bodies of troops in these expeditions, which he considered as a sort of substitute for war.

He required that none of the natives of the country should be employed as servants, or allowed to perform any menial duties whatever. For these purposes the people were required to depend on captives taken in war and enslaved. One reason why he made this rule was to stimulate the people on the frontiers to make hostile excursions among their neighbors, in order to supply themselves and the country generally with slaves.

The right of property in the slaves thus taken was very strictly guarded, and very severe laws were made to enforce it. It was forbidden, on pain of death, to harbor a slave, or give him meat or drink, clothing or shelter, without permission from his master. The penalty was death, too, if a person meeting a fugitive slave neglected to seize and secure him, and deliver him to his master.

Every man could marry as many wives as he pleased, and his female slaves were all, by law, entirely at his disposal to be made concubines.

There was one very curious arrangement, which grew out of the great importance which, as we have already seen, was attached to the ties of relationship and family connection among these pastoral nations. Two families could bind themselves together and make themselves legally one, in respect to their connection, by a fictitious marriage arranged between children no longer living. In such a case the contracts were regularly made, just as if the children were still alive, and the ceremonies were all duly performed. After this the two families were held to be legally allied, and they were bound to each other by all the obligations which would have arisen in the case of a real marriage. This custom is said to be continued among some of the Tartar nations to the present day. The people think, it is said, that such a wedding ceremony, duly solemnized by the parents of children who are dead, takes effect upon the subjects of it in the world of spirits, and that thus their union, though arranged and consecrated on earth, is confirmed and consummated in heaven.

Besides these peculiar and special enactments, there were the ordinary laws against robbery, theft, murder, adultery, and false witness. The penalties for these offenses were generally severe. The punishment for stealing cattle was death. For petty thefts the criminal was to be beaten with a stick, the number of the blows being proportioned to the nature and aggravation of the offense. He could, however, if he had the means, buy himself off from this punishment by paying nine times the value of the thing stolen.

In respect to religion, the constitution which Temujin made declared that there was but one God, the creator of heaven and earth, and it acknowledged him as the supreme ruler and governor of all mankind, the being "who alone gives life and death, riches and poverty, who grants and denies whatever he pleases, and exercises over all things an absolute power." This one fundamental article of faith was all that was required. For the rest, Temujin left the various nations and tribes throughout his dominions to adopt such modes of worship and to celebrate such religious rites as they severally preferred, and forbade that any one should be disturbed or molested in any way on account of his religion, whatever form it might assume.

At length the time arrived for the grand assembly of the khans to be convened. The meeting was called, not at Karakorom, the capital, but at a central spot in the interior of the country, called Dilon Ildak. Such a spot was much more convenient than any town or city would have been for the place of meeting, on account of the great troops of horses and the herds of animals by which the khans were always accompanied in all their expeditions, and which made it necessary that, whenever any considerable number of them were to be convened, the place chosen should be suitable for a grand encampment, with extensive and fertile pasture-grounds extending all around.

As the several khans came in, each at the head of his own troop of retainers and followers, they severally chose their ground, pitched their tents, and turned their herds of horses, sheep, and oxen out to pasture on the plains. Thus, in the course of a few days, the whole country in every direction became dotted with villages of tents, among which groups of horsemen were now and then to be seen galloping to and fro, and small herds of cattle, each under the care of herdsmen and slaves, moved slowly, cropping the grass as they advanced along the hill-sides and through the valleys.

At length, when all had assembled, a spot was selected in the centre of the encampment for the performance of the ceremonies. A raised seat was prepared for Temujin in a situation suitable to enable him to address the assembly from it. Before and around this the various khans and their attendants and followers gathered, and Temujin made them an oration, in which he explained the circumstances under which they had come together, and announced to them his plans and intentions in respect to the future. He stated to them that, in consequence of the victories which he had gained through their co-operation and assistance, the foundation of a great empire had been laid, and that he had now called them together in order that they might join with him in organizing the requisite government for such a dominion, and in electing a prince or sovereign to rule over it. He called upon them first to proceed to the election of this ruler.

The khans accordingly proceeded to the election. This was, in fact, only a form, for Temujin himself was, of course, to be chosen. The election was, however, made, and one of the oldest and most venerable of the khans was commissioned to announce the result. He came forward with great solemnity, and, in the presence of the whole assembly, declared that the choice had fallen upon Temujin. He then made an address to Temujin himself, who was seated during this part of the ceremony upon a carpet of black felt spread upon the ground. In the address the khan reminded Temujin that the exalted authority with which he was now invested came from God, and that to God he was responsible for the right exercise of his power. If he governed his subjects well, God, he said, would render his reign prosperous and happy; but if, on the other hand, he abused his power, he would come to a miserable end.

After the conclusion of the address, seven of the khans, who had been designated for this purpose, came and lifted Temujin up and bore him away to a throne which had been set up for him in the midst of the assembly, where all the khans, and their various bodies of attendants, came and offered him their homage.

Among others there came a certain old prophet, named Kokza, who was held in great veneration by all the people on account of his supposed inspiration and the austere life which he led. He used to go very thinly clad, and with his feet bare summer and winter, and it was supposed that his power of enduring the exposures to which he was thus subject was something miraculous and divine. He had received accordingly from the people a name which signified _the image of God_, and he was everywhere looked upon as inspired. He said, moreover, that a white horse came to him from time to time and carried him up to heaven, where he conversed face to face with God, and received the revelations which he was commissioned to make to men. All this the people fully believed. The man may have been an impostor, or he may have been insane. Oftentimes, in such cases, the inspiration which the person supposes he is the subject of arises from a certain spiritual exaltation, which, though it does not wholly unfit him for the ordinary avocations and duties of life, still verges upon insanity, and often finally lapses into it entirely.

This old prophet advanced toward Temujin while he was seated on his carpet of felt, and made a solemn address to him in the hearing of all the assembled khans. He was charged, he said, with a message from heaven in respect to the kingdom and dominion of Temujin, which had been, he declared, ordained of God, and had now been established in fulfillment of the Divine will. He was commissioned, moreover, he said, to give to Temujin the style and title of Genghis Khan,[D] and to declare that his kingdom should not only endure while he lived, but should descend to his posterity, from generation to generation, to the remotest times.

[Footnote D: The signification of these words, in the language of the Monguls, was _great khan of khans_.]

The people, on hearing this address, at once adopted the name which the prophet had given to their new ruler, and saluted Temujin with it in long and loud acclamations. It was thus that our hero received the name of Genghis Khan, which soon extended its fame through every part of Asia, and has since become so greatly renowned through all the world.

*   *   *   *   *

Temujin, or Genghis Khan, as we must now henceforth call him, having thus been proclaimed by the acclamations of the people under the new title with which the old prophet had invested him, sat upon his throne while his subjects came to render him their homage. First the khans themselves came up, and kneeled nine times before him, in token of their absolute and complete submission to his authority. After they had retired the people themselves came, and made their obeisance in the same manner. As they rose from their knees after the last prostration, they made the air resound once more with their shouts, crying "Long live great Genghis Khan!" in repeated and prolonged acclamations.

After this the new emperor made what might be called his inaugural address. The khans and their followers gathered once more before his throne while he delivered an oration to them, in which he thanked them for the honor which they had done him in raising him to the supreme power, and announced to them the principles by which he should be guided in the government of his empire. He promised to be just in his dealings with his subjects, and also to be merciful. He would defend them, he said, against all their enemies. He would do everything in his power to promote their comfort and happiness. He would lead them to honor and glory, and would make their names known throughout the earth. He would deal impartially, too, with all the different tribes and hordes, and would treat the Monguls and the Tartars, the two great classes of his subjects, with equal favor.

When the speech was concluded Genghis Khan distributed presents to all the subordinate khans, both great and small. He also made magnificent entertainments, which were continued for several days. After thus spending some time in feasting and rejoicings, the khans one after another took their leave of the emperor, the great encampment was broken up, and the different tribes set out on their return to their several homes.

CHAPTER 12: DOMINIONS OF GENGHIS KHAN
1203

Karakorom—Insignificance of cities and towns—Account of Karakorom—The buildings—The grand encampments—Construction of the tents—Dwellings of the women—Mountains and wild beasts—Hunting—The danger of hunting in those days—Modern weapons—Carabines—Fulminating balls—Devisme's establishment in Paris—Specimens—Great danger—Wild beasts more formidable than men—Grand huntsman—Timid animals—Stratagems—Mode of taking deer—Training of the horses—Great desert—Cold—No forests—Pasturage—Burning the grass on the plains.

After the ceremonies of the inauguration were concluded, Genghis Khan returned, with the officers of his court and his immediate followers, to Karakorom. This town, though nominally the capital of the empire, was, after all, quite an insignificant place. Indeed, but little importance was attached to any villages or towns in those days, and there were very few fixed places of residence that were of any considerable account. The reason is, that towns are the seats of commerce and manufactures, and they derive their chief importance from those pursuits; whereas the Monguls and Tartars led almost exclusively a wandering and pastoral life, and all their ideas of wealth and grandeur were associated with great flocks and herds of cattle, and handsome tents, and long trains of wagons loaded with stores of clothing, arms, and other movables, and vast encampments in the neighborhood of rich and extended pasture-grounds. Those who lived permanently in fixed houses they looked down upon as an inferior class, confined to one spot by their poverty or their toil, while they themselves could roam at liberty with their flocks and herds over the plains, riding fleet horses or dromedaries, and encamping where they pleased in the green valleys or on the banks of the meandering streams.

Karakorom was accordingly by no means a great and splendid city. It was surrounded by what was called a mud wall—that is, a wall made of blocks of clay dried in the sun. The houses of the inhabitants were mere hovels, and even the palace of the king, and all the other public buildings, were of very frail construction; for all the architecture of the Monguls in those days took its character from the tent, which was the type and model, so to speak, of all other buildings.

The new emperor, however, did not spend a great deal of his time at Karakorom. He was occupied for some years in making excursions at the head of his troops to various parts of his dominions, for the purpose of putting down insurrections, overawing discontented and insubordinate khans, and settling disputes of various kinds arising between the different hordes. In these expeditions he was accustomed to move by easy marches across the plains at the head of his army, and sometimes would establish himself in a sort of permanent camp, where he would remain, perhaps, as in a fixed residence, for weeks or months at a time.

Not only Genghis Khan himself, but many of the other great chieftains, were accustomed to live in this manner, and one of their encampments, if we could have seen it, would have been regarded by us as a great curiosity. The ground was regularly laid out, like a town, into quarters, squares, and streets, and the space which it covered was sometimes so large as to extend nearly a mile in each direction. The tent of the khan himself was in the centre. A space was reserved for it there large enough not only for the grand tent itself, but also for the rows of smaller tents near, for the wives and for other women belonging to the khan's family, and also for the rows of carts or wagons containing the stores of provisions, the supplies of clothing and arms, and the other valuables which these wandering chieftains always took with them in all their peregrinations.

The tent of the khan in summer was made of a sort of calico, and in winter of felt, which was much warmer. It was raised very high, so as to be seen above all the rest of the encampment, and it was painted in gay colors, and adorned with other barbaric decorations.

The dwellings in which the women were lodged, which were around or near the great tent, were sometimes tents, and sometimes little huts made of wood. When they were of wood they were made very light, and were constructed in such a manner that they could be taken to pieces at the shortest notice, and packed on carts or wagons, in order to be transported to the next place of encampment, whenever, for any reason, it became necessary for their lord and master to remove his domicile to a different ground.

A large portion of the country which was included within the limits of Genghis Khan's dominions was fertile ground, which produced abundance of grass for the pasturage of the flocks and herds, and many springs and streams of water. There were, however, several districts of mountainous country, which were the refuge of tigers, leopards, wolves, and other ferocious beasts of prey. It was among these mountains that the great hunting parties which Genghis Khan organized from time to time went in search of their game. There was a great officer of the kingdom, called the grand huntsman, who had the superintendence and charge of everything relating to hunting and to game throughout the empire. The grand huntsman was an officer of the very highest rank. He even took precedence of the first ministers of state. Genghis Khan appointed his son Jughi, who has already been mentioned in connection with the great council of war called by his father, and with the battle which was subsequently fought, and in which he gained great renown, to the office of grand huntsman, and, at the same time, made two of the older and more experienced khans his ministers of state.

The hunting of wild beasts as ferocious as those that infested the mountains of Asia is a very dangerous amusement even at the present day, notwithstanding the advantage which the huntsman derives from the use of gunpowder, and rifled barrels, and fulminating bullets. But in those days, when the huntsman had no better weapons than bows and arrows, javelins, and spears, the undertaking was dangerous in the extreme. An African lion of full size used to be considered as a match for _forty_ men in the days when only ordinary weapons were used against him, and it was considered almost hopeless to attack him with less than that number. And even with that number to waylay and assail him he was not usually conquered until he had killed or disabled two or three of his foes.

Now, however, with the terrible artillery invented in modern times, a single man, if he has the requisite courage, coolness, and steadiness of nerve, is a match for such a lion. The weapon used is a double-barreled carabine, both barrels being _rifled_, that is, provided with spiral grooves within, that operate to give the bullets a rotary motion as they issue from the muzzle, by which they bore their way through the air, as it were, to their destination, with a surprising directness and precision. The bullets discharged by these carabines are not balls, but cylinders, pointed with a cone at the forward end. They are hollow, and are filled with a fulminating composition which is capable of exploding with a force vastly greater than that of gunpowder. The conical point at the end is made separate from the body of the cylinder, and slides into it by a sort of shank, which, when the bullet strikes the body of the lion or other wild beast, acts like a sort of percussion cap to explode the fulminating powder, and thus the instant that the missile enters the animal's body it bursts with a terrible explosion, and scatters the iron fragments of the cylinder among his vitals. Thus, while an ordinary musket ball might lodge in his flesh, or even pass entirely through some parts of his body, without producing any other effect than to arouse him to a phrensy, and redouble the force with which he would spring upon his foe, the bursting of one of these fulminating bullets almost anywhere within his body brings him down in an instant, and leaves him writhing and rolling upon the ground in the agonies of death.

On the Boulevard des Italians, in Paris, is the manufactory of Devisme, who makes these carabines for the lion-hunters of Algiers. Promenaders, in passing by his windows, stop to look at specimens of these bullets exhibited there. They are of various sizes, adapted to barrels of different bores. Some are entire; others are rent and torn in pieces, having been fired into a bank of earth, that they might burst there as they would do in the body of a wild beast, and then be recovered and preserved to show the effect of the explosion.

Even with such terrible weapons as these, it requires at the present day great courage, great coolness, and very extraordinary steadiness of nerve to face a lion or a tiger in his mountain fastness, with any hope of coming off victorious in the contest. But the danger was, of course, infinitely greater in the days of Genghis Khan, when pikes and spears, and bows and arrows, were the only weapons with which the body of huntsmen could arm themselves for the combat. Indeed, in those days wild beasts were even in some respects more formidable enemies than men. For men, however excited by angry passions, are, in some degree, under the influence of fear. They will not rush headlong upon absolute and certain destruction, but may be driven back by a mere display of force, if it is obvious that it is a force which they are wholly incapable of resisting. Thus a party of men, however desperate, may be attacked without much danger to the assailants, provided that the force which the assailants bring against them is overwhelming.

But it is not so with wild beasts. A lion, a tiger, or a panther, once aroused, is wholly insensible to fear. He will rush headlong upon his foes, however numerous they may be, and however formidably armed. He makes his own destruction sure, it is true, but, at the same time, he renders almost inevitable the destruction of some one or more of his enemies, and, in going out to attack him, no one can be sure of not becoming himself one of the victims of his fury.

Thus the hunting of wild beasts in the mountains was very dangerous work, and it is not surprising that the office of grand huntsman was one of great consideration and honor.

The hunting was, however, not all of the dangerous character above described. Some animals are timid and inoffensive by nature, and attempt to save themselves only by flight. Such animals as these were to be pursued and overtaken by the superior speed of horses and dogs, or to be circumvented by stratagem. There was a species of deer, in certain parts of the Mongul country, that the huntsmen were accustomed to take in this way, namely:

The huntsmen, when they began to draw near to a place where a herd of deer were feeding, would divide themselves into two parties. One party would provide themselves with the antlers of stags, which they arranged in such a manner that they could hold them up over their heads in the thickets, as if real stags were there. The others, armed with bows and arrows, javelins, spears, and other such weapons, would place themselves in ambush near by. Those who had the antlers would then make a sort of cry, imitating that uttered by the hinds. The stags of the herd, hearing the cry, would immediately come toward the spot. The men in the thicket then would raise the antlers and move them about, so as to deceive the stags, and excite their feelings of rivalry and ire, while those who were appointed to that office continued to counterfeit the cry of the hind. The stags immediately would begin to paw the ground and to prepare for a conflict, and then, while their attention was thus wholly taken up by the tossing of the false antlers in the thicket, the men in ambush would creep up as near as they could, take good aim, and shoot their poor deluded victims through the heart.

Of course, it required a great deal of practice and much skill to perform successfully such feats as these; and there were many other branches of the huntsman's art, as practiced in those days, which could only be acquired by a systematic and special course of training. One of the most difficult things was to train the horses so that they would advance to meet tigers and other wild beasts without fear. Horses have naturally a strong and instinctive terror for such beasts, and this terror it was very difficult to overcome. The Mongul huntsmen, however, contrived means to inspire the horses with so much courage in this respect that they would advance to the encounter of these terrible foes with as much ardor as a trained charger shows in advancing to meet other horses and horsemen on the field of battle.

Besides the mountainous regions above described, there were several deserts in the country of the Monguls. The greatest of these deserts extends through the very heart of Asia, and is one of the most extensive districts of barren land in the world. Unlike most other great deserts, however, the land is very elevated, and it is to this elevation that its barrenness is, in a great measure, due. A large part of this desert consists of rocks and barren sands, and, in the time of which we are writing, was totally uninhabitable. It was so cold, too, on account of the great elevation of the land, that it was almost impossible to traverse it except in the warmest season of the year.

Other parts of this district, which were not so elevated, and where the land was not quite so barren, produced grass and herbage on which the flocks and herds could feed, and thus, in certain seasons of the year, people resorted to them for pasturage.

Throughout the whole country there were no extensive forests. There were a few tangled thickets among the mountains, where the wild beasts concealed themselves and made their lairs, but this was all. One reason why forests did not spring up was, as is supposed, the custom of the people to burn over the plains every spring, as the Indians were accustomed to do on the American prairies. In the spring the dead grass of the preceding year lay dry and withered, and sometimes closely matted together, on the ground, thus hindering, as the people thought, the fresh grass from growing up. So the people were accustomed, on some spring morning when there was a good breeze blowing, to set it on fire. The fire would run rapidly over the plains, burning up everything in its way that was above the ground. But the roots of the grass, being below, were safe from it. Very soon afterward the new grass would spring up with great luxuriance. The people thought that the rich verdure which the new grass displayed, and its subsequent rapid growth, were owing simply to the fact that the old dead grass was out of the way. It is now known, however, that the burning of the old grass leaves an ash upon the ground which acts powerfully as a fertilizer, and that the richness of the fresh vegetation is due, in a great measure, to this cause.

Such was the country which was inhabited by the wandering pastoral tribes that were now under the sway of Genghis Khan. His dominion had no settled boundaries, for it was a dominion over certain tribes rather than over a certain district of country. Nearly all the tribes composing both the Mongul and the Tartar nations had now submitted to him, though he still had some small wars to wage from time to time with some of the more distant tribes before his authority was fully and finally acknowledged. The history of some of these conflicts will be narrated in the next chapter.

CHAPTER 13: ADVENTURES OF PRINCE KUSHLUK
1203-1208

Kushluk's escape—Tukta Bey—Kashin—Temujin pursues Tukta Bey and Kushluk—Retreat to Boyrak's country——The various tribes submit—Fall and destruction of Kashin—Proclamation—Temujin returns to Karakorom—Boyrak's precautions—Great battle—Boyrak is taken and slain—Flight of Kushluk and Tukta Bey—Ardish—River Irtish—Tukta Bey's adherents—Genghis Khan pursues them in winter—Difficulties of the country—Death of Tukta Bey—Kushluk escapes again—Turkestan—He is received by Gurkhan—Presentation of the _shongar_—Urus Inal.

Prince Kushluk, as the reader will perhaps recollect, was the son of Tayian, the khan of the Naymans, who organized the grand league of khans against Temujin at the instigation of Yemuka, as related in a preceding chapter. He was the young prince who was opposed to Jughi, the son of Temujin, in the great final battle. The reader will recollect that in that battle Tayian himself was slain, as was also Yemuka, but the young prince succeeded in making his escape.

He was accompanied in his flight by a certain general or chieftain named Tukta Bey. This Tukta Bey was the khan of a powerful tribe. The name of the town or village which he considered his capital was Kashin. It was situated toward the southwest, not far from the borders of China. Tukta Bey, taking Kushluk with him, retreated to this place, and there began to make preparations to collect a new army to act against Temujin. I say Temujin, for these circumstances took place immediately after the battle, and before Temujin had received his new title of Genghis Khan.

Temujin, having learned that Tukta Bey and the young prince had gone to Kashin, determined at once to follow them there. As soon as Tukta Bey heard that he was coming, he began to strengthen the fortifications of his town and to increase the garrison. He also laid in supplies of food and military stores of all kinds. While he was making these preparations, he received the news that Temujin was advancing into his country at the head of an immense force. The force was so large that he was convinced that his town could not long stand out against it. He was greatly perplexed to know what to do.

Now it happened that there was a brother of Tayian Khan's, named Boyrak, the chief of a powerful horde that occupied a district of country not very far distant from Tukta Bey's dominions. Tukta Bey thought that this Boyrak would be easily induced to aid him in the war, as it was a war waged against the mortal enemy of his brother. He determined to leave his capital to be defended by the garrison which he had placed in it, and to proceed himself to Boyrak's country to obtain re-enforcements. He first sent off the Prince Kushluk, so that he might be as soon as possible in a place of safety. Then, after completing the necessary arrangements and dispositions for the defense of his town, in case it should be attacked during his absence, he took his oldest son, for whose safety he was also greatly concerned, and set out at the head of a small troop of horsemen to go to Boyrak.

Accordingly, when Temujin, at the head of his forces, arrived at the town of Kashin, he found that the fugitives whom he was pursuing were no longer there. However, he determined to take the town. He accordingly at once invested it, and commenced the siege. The garrison made a very determined resistance. But the forces under Temujin's command were too strong for them. The town was soon taken. Temujin ordered his soldiers to slay without mercy all who were found in arms against him within the walls, and the walls themselves, and all the other defenses of the place, he caused to be leveled with the ground.

He then issued his proclamation, offering peace and pardon to all the rest of the tribe on condition that they would take the oath of allegiance to him. This they readily agreed to do. There were a great many subordinate khans, both of this tribe and of some others that were near, who thus yielded to Temujin, and promised to obey him.

All this took place, as has already been said, immediately after the great battle with Tayian, and before Temujin had been enthroned as emperor, or had received his new title of Genghis Khan. Indeed, Temujin, while making this expedition to Kashin in pursuit of Kushluk and Tukta Bey, had been somewhat uneasy at the loss of time which the campaign occasioned him, as he was anxious to go as soon as possible to Karakorom, in order to take the necessary measures there for arranging and consolidating his government. He accordingly now determined not to pursue the fugitives any farther, but to proceed at once to Karakorom, and postpone all farther operations against Kushluk and Tukta until the next season. So he went to Karakorom, and there, during the course of the winter, formed the constitution of his new empire, and made arrangements for convening a grand assembly of the khans the next spring, as related in the last chapter.

In the mean time, Tukta Bey and the Prince Kushluk were very kindly received by Boyrak, Tayian's brother. For a time they all had reason to expect that Temujin, after having taken and destroyed Kashin, would continue his pursuit of the prince, and Boyrak began accordingly to make preparations for defense. But when, at length, they learned that Temujin had given up the pursuit, and had returned to Karakorom, their apprehensions were, for the moment, relieved. They were, however, well aware that the danger was only postponed; and Boyrak, being determined to defend the cause of his nephew, and to avenge, if possible, his brother's death, occupied himself diligently with increasing his army, strengthening his fortifications, and providing himself with all possible means of defense against the attack which he expected would be made upon him in the coming season.

Boyrak's expectations of an attack were fully realized. Temujin, after having settled the affairs of his government, and having now become Genghis Khan, took the first opportunity in the following season to fit out an expedition against Tukta Bey and Boyrak. He marched into Boyrak's dominions at the head of a strong force. Boyrak came forth to meet him. A great battle was fought. Boyrak was entirely defeated. When he found that the battle was lost he attempted to fly. He was, however, pursued and taken, and was then brought back to the camp of Genghis Khan, where he was put to death. The conqueror undoubtedly justified this act of cruelty toward his helpless prisoner on the plea that, like Yemuka, he was not an open and honorable foe, but a rebel and traitor, and, consequently, that the act of putting him to death was the execution of a criminal, and not the murder of a prisoner.

But, although Boyrak himself was thus taken and slain, Kushluk and Tukta Bey succeeded in making their escape. They fled to the northward and westward, scarcely knowing, it would seem, where they were to go. They at last found a place of refuge on the banks of the River Irtish. This river rises not far from the centre of the Asiatic continent, and flows northward into the Northern Ocean. The country through which it flows lay to the northwestward of Genghis Khan's dominions, and beyond the confines of it. Through this country Prince Kushluk and Tukta Bey wandered on, accompanied by the small troop of followers that still adhered to them, until they reached a certain fortress called Ardish, where they determined to make a stand.

They were among friends here, for Ardish, it seems, was on the confines of territory that belonged to Tukta Bey. The people of the neighborhood immediately flocked to Tukta's standard, and thus the fugitive khan soon found himself at the head of a considerable force. This force was farther increased by the coming in of broken bands that had made their escape from the battle at which Boyrak had been slain at the same time with Tukta Bey, but had become separated from him in their flight.

It would seem that, at first, Genghis Khan did not know what was become of the fugitives. At any rate, it was not until the next year that he attempted to pursue them. Then, hearing where they were and what they were doing, he prepared an expedition to penetrate into the country of the Irtish and attack them. It was in the dead of winter when he arrived in the country. He had hurried on at that season of the year in order to prevent Tukta Bey from having time to finish his fortifications. Tukta Bey and those who were with him were amazed when they heard that their enemy was coming at that season of the year. The defenses which they were preparing for their fortress were not fully completed, but they were at once convinced that they could not hold their ground against the body of troops that Genghis Khan was bringing against them in the open field, and so they all took shelter in and near the fortress, and awaited their enemy there.

The winters in that latitude are very cold, and the country through which Genghis Khan had to march was full of difficulty. The branches of the river which he had to cross were obstructed with ice, and the roads were in many places rendered almost impassable by snow. The emperor did not even know the way to the fortress where Tukta Bey and his followers were concealed, and it would have been almost impossible for him to find it had it not been for certain tribes, through whose territories he passed on the way, who furnished him with guides. These tribes, perceiving how overwhelming was the force which Genghis Khan commanded, knew that it would be useless for them to resist him. So they yielded submission to him at once, and detached parties of horsemen to go with him down the river to show him the way.

Under the conduct of these guides Genghis Khan passed on. In due time he arrived at the fortress of Ardish, and immediately forced Tukta Bey and his allies to come to an engagement. Tukta's army was very soon defeated and put to flight. Tukta himself, and many other khans and chieftains who had joined him, were killed; but the Prince Kushluk was once more fortunate enough to make his escape.

He fled with a small troop of followers, all mounted on fleet horses, and after various wanderings, in the course of which he and they who were with him endured a great deal of privation and suffering, the unhappy fugitive at last reached the dominions of a powerful prince named Gurkhan, who reigned over a country which is situated in the western part of Asia, toward the Caspian Sea, and is named Turkestan. This is the country from which the people called the Turks, who afterward spread themselves so widely over the western part of Asia and the eastern part of Europe, originally sprung.

Gurkhan received Kushluk and his party in a very friendly manner, and Genghis Khan did not follow them. Whether he thought that the distance was too great, or that the power of Gurkhan was too formidable to make it prudent for him to advance into his dominions without a stronger force, does not appear. At any rate, for the time being he gave up the pursuit, and after fully securing the fruits of the victory which he had gained at Ardish, and receiving the submission of all the tribes and khans that inhabited that region of country, he set out on his return home.

It is related that one of the khans who gave in his submission to Genghis Khan at this time made him a present of a certain bird called a _shongar_, according to a custom often observed among the people of that region. The shongar was a very large and fierce bird of prey, which, however, could be trained like the falcons which were so much prized in the Middle Ages by the princes and nobles of Europe. It seems it was customary for an inferior khan to present one of these birds to his superior on great occasions, as an emblem and token of his submission to his superior's authority. The bird in such a case was very richly decorated with gold and precious stones, so that the present was sometimes of a very costly and magnificent character.

Genghis Khan received such a present as this from a chieftain named Urus Inal, who was among those that yielded to his sway in the country of the Irtish, after the battle at which Tukta Bey was defeated and killed. The bird was presented to Genghis Khan by Urus with great ceremony, as an act of submission and homage.

What, in the end, was the fate of Prince Kushluk, will appear in the next chapter.

PRESENTATION OF THE SHONGAR.

81

CHAPTER 14: IDIKUT
1208

Idikut—The old system of farming revenues—Evils of farming the revenue—Modern system—Disinterested collectors—Independent and impartial courts—Waste of the public money—Shuwakem—Idikut's quarrel with Gurkhan's tax-gatherers—Rebellion—He sends to Genghis Khan—His reception of the embassy—Idikut's visit to Genghis Khan—Gurkhan in a rage—Jena—Subsequent history of Kushluk—Kushluk's final defeat and flight—Hotly pursued by Jena—Kushluk's death—Genghis Khan's triumph.

There was another great and powerful khan, named Idikut, whose tribe had hitherto been under the dominion of Gurkhan, the Prince of Turkestan, where Kushluk had sought refuge, but who about this time revolted from Gurkhan and went over to Genghis Khan, under circumstances which illustrate, in some degree, the peculiar nature of the political ties by which these different tribes and nations were bound to each other. It seems that the tribe over which Idikut ruled was tributary to Turkestan, and that Gurkhan had an officer stationed in Idikut's country whose business it was to collect and remit the tribute. The name of this collector was Shuwakem. He was accustomed, it seems, like almost all tax-gatherers in those days, to exact more than was his due. The system generally adopted by governments in that age of the world for collecting their revenues from tributary or conquered provinces was to _farm them_, as the phrase was. That is, they sold the whole revenue of a particular district in the gross to some rich man, who paid for it a specific sum, considerably less, of course, than the tax itself would really yield, and then he reimbursed himself for his outlay and for his trouble by collecting the tax in detail from the people. Of course, it was for the interest of the tax-gatherer, in such a case, after having paid the round sum to the government, to extort as much as possible from the people, since all that he obtained over and above the sum that he had paid was his profit on the transaction. Then, if the people complained to the government of his exactions, they could seldom obtain any redress, for the government knew that if they rebuked or punished the farmer of the revenue, or interfered with him in any way, they would not be able to make so favorable terms with him for the next year.

The plan of farming the revenues thus led to a great deal of extortion and oppression, which the people were compelled patiently to endure, as there was generally no remedy. In modern times and among civilized nations this system has been almost universally abandoned. The taxes are now always collected for the government directly by officers who have to pay over not a fixed sum, but simply what they collect. Thus the tax-gatherers are, in some sense, impartial, since, if they collect more than the law entitles them to demand, the benefit inures almost wholly to the government, they themselves gaining little or no advantage by their extortion. Besides this, there are courts established which are, in a great measure, independent of the government, to which the tax-payer can appeal at once in a case where he thinks he is aggrieved. This, it is true, often puts him to a great deal of trouble and expense, but, in the end, he is pretty sure to have justice done him, while under the old system there was ordinarily no remedy at all. There was nothing to be done but to appeal to the king or chieftain himself, and these complaints seldom received any attention. For, besides the natural unwillingness of the sovereign to trouble himself about such disputes, he had a direct interest in not requiring the extorted money to be paid back, or, rather, in not having it proved that it was extorted. Thus the poor tax-payer found that the officer who collected the money, and the umpire who was to decide in case of disputes, were both directly interested against him, and he was continually wronged; whereas, at the present day, by means of a system which provides disinterested officers to determine and collect the tax, and independent judges to decide all cases of dispute, the evils are almost wholly avoided. The only difficulty now is the extravagance and waste with which the public money is expended, making it necessary to collect a much larger amount than would otherwise be required. Perhaps some future generation will discover some plain and simple remedy for this evil too.

*   *   *   *   *

The name of the officer who had the general charge of the collection of the taxes in Idikut's territory for Gurkhan, King of Turkestan, was, as has already been said, Shuwakem. He oppressed the people, exacting more from them than was really due. Whether he had farmed the revenue, and was thus enriching himself by his extortions, or whether he was acting directly in Gurkhan's name, and made the people pay more than he ought from zeal in his master's service, and a desire to recommend himself to favor by sending home to Turkestan as large a revenue from the provinces as possible, does not appear. At all events, the people complained bitterly. They had, however, no access to Gurkhan, Shuwakem's master, and so they carried their complaints to Idikut, their own khan.

Idikut remonstrated with Shuwakem, but he, instead of taking the remonstrance in good part and relaxing the severity of his proceedings, resented the interference of Idikut, and answered him in a haughty and threatening manner. This made Idikut very angry. Indeed, he was angry before, as it might naturally be supposed that he would have been, at having a person owing allegiance to a foreign prince exercising authority in a proud and domineering manner within his dominions, and the reply which Shuwakem made when he remonstrated with him on account of his extortions exasperated him beyond all bounds. He immediately caused Shuwakem to be assassinated. He also slew all the other officers of Gurkhan within his country—those, probably, who were employed to assist Shuwakem in collecting the taxes.

The murder of these officers was, of course, an act of open rebellion against Gurkhan, and Idikut, in order to shield himself from the consequences of it, determined to join himself and his tribe at once to the empire of Genghis Khan; so he immediately dispatched two ambassadors to the Mongul emperor with his proposals.

The envoys, accompanied by a suitable troop of guards and attendants, went into the Mongul country and presently came up with Genghis Khan, while he was on a march toward the country of some tribe or horde that had revolted from him. They were very kindly received; for, although Genghis Khan was not prepared at present to make open war upon Gurkhan, or to invade his dominions in pursuit of Prince Kushluk, he was intending to do this at some future day, and, in the mean time, he was very glad to weaken his enemy by drawing off from his empire any tributary tribes that were at all disposed to revolt from him.

He accordingly received the ambassadors of Idikut in a very cordial and friendly manner. He readily acceded to the proposals which Idikut made through them, and, in order to give full proof to Idikut of the readiness and sincerity with which he accepted his proposals, he sent back two ambassadors of his own to accompany Idikut's ambassadors on their return, and to join them in assuring that prince of the cordiality with which Genghis Khan accepted his offers of friendship, and to promise his protection.

Idikut was very much pleased, when his messengers returned, to learn that his mission had been so successful. He immediately determined to go himself and visit Genghis Khan in his camp, in order to confirm the new alliance by making a personal tender to the emperor of his homage and his services. He accordingly prepared some splendid presents, and, placing himself at the head of his troop of guards, he proceeded to the camp of Genghis Khan. The emperor received him in a very kind and friendly manner. He accepted his presents, and, in the end, was so much pleased with Idikut himself that he gave him one of his daughters in marriage.

As for Gurkhan, when he first heard of the murder of Shuwakem and the other officers, he was in a terrible rage. He declared that he would revenge his servant by laying waste Idikut's territories with fire and sword. But when he heard that Idikut had placed himself under the protection of Genghis Khan, and especially when he learned that he had married the emperor's daughter, he thought it more prudent to postpone his vengeance, not being quite willing to draw upon himself the hostility of so great a power.

Prince Kushluk remained for many years in Turkestan and in the countries adjoining it. He married a daughter of Gurkhan, his protector. Partly in consequence of this connection and of the high rank which he had held in his own native land, and partly, perhaps, in consequence of his personal courage and other military qualities, he rapidly acquired great influence among the khans of Western Asia, and at last he organized a sort of rebellion against Gurkhan, made war against him, and deprived him of more than half his dominions. He then collected a large army, and prepared to make war upon Genghis Khan. Genghis Khan sent one of his best generals, at the head of a small but very compact and well-disciplined force, against him. The name of this general was Jena. Kushluk was not at all intimidated by the danger which now threatened him. His own army was much larger than that of Jena, and he accordingly advanced to meet his enemy without fear. He was, however, beaten in the battle, and, when he saw that the day was lost, he fled, followed by a small party of horsemen, who succeeded in saving themselves with him.

Jena set out immediately in pursuit of the fugitive, accompanied by a small body of men mounted on the fleetest horses. The party who were with Kushluk, being exhausted by the fatigue of the battle and bewildered by the excitement and terror of their flight, could not keep together, but were overtaken one by one and slain by their pursuers until only three were left. These three kept close to Kushluk, and with him went on until Jena's party lost the track of them.

At length, coming to a place where two roads met, Jena asked a peasant if he had seen any strange horsemen pass that way. The peasant said that four horsemen had passed a short time before, and he told Jena which road they had taken.

Jena and his party rode on in the direction which the peasant had indicated, and, pushing forward with redoubled speed, they soon overtook the unhappy fugitives. They fell upon Kushluk without mercy, and killed him on the spot. They then cut off his head, and turned back to carry it to Genghis Khan.

Genghis Khan rewarded Jena in the most magnificent manner for his successful performance of this exploit, and then, putting Kushluk's head upon a pole, he displayed it in all the camps and villages through which he passed, where it served at once as a token and a trophy of his victory against an enemy, and, at the same time, as a warning to all other persons of the terrible danger which they would incur in attempting to resist his power.

CHAPTER 15: THE STORY OF HUJAKU
1211

China—The Chinese wall—The frontier—Outside the wall—Origin of the quarrel with the Chinese—Yong-tsi—Genghis Khan's contempt for him—Armies raised—Hujaku—Many of the khans come over on Genghis's side—Victory over Hujaku—Genghis Khan is wounded—Hujaku disgraced—Restored again—Dissensions among the Chinese—Advance of the Monguls—Hujaku's rebellion—Death of Yong-tsi—Hujaku advances—The battle—Hujaku's victory—Kan-ki's expedition—Hujaku enraged—Failure—Kan-ki's second trial—The sand-storm—Kan-ki's desperate resolution—The attack—Hujaku's flight—He is killed in the gardens—Kan-ki is pardoned and promoted.

The accounts given us of the events and transactions of Genghis Khan's reign after he acquired the supreme power over the Mongul and Tartar nations are imperfect, and, in many respects, confused. It appears, however, from them that in the year 1211, that is, about five years after his election as grand khan, he became involved in a war with the Chinese, which led, in the end, to very important consequences. The kingdom of China lay to the southward of the Mongul territories, and the frontier was defended by the famous Chinese wall, which extended from east to west, over hills and valleys, from the great desert to the sea, for many hundred miles. The wall was defended by towers, built here and there in commanding positions along the whole extent of it, and at certain distances there were fortified towns where powerful garrisons were stationed, and reserves of troops were held ready to be marched to different points along the wall, wherever there might be occasion for their services.

The wall was not strictly the Chinese frontier, for the territory on the outside of it to a considerable distance was held by the Chinese government, and there were many large towns and some very strong fortresses in this outlying region, all of which were held and garrisoned by Chinese troops.

The inhabitants, however, of the countries outside the wall were generally of the Tartar or Mongul race. They were of a nation or tribe called _the Kitan_, and were somewhat inclined to rebel against the Chinese rule. In order to assist in keeping them in subjection, one of the Chinese emperors issued a decree which ordained that the governors of those provinces should place in all the large towns, and other strongholds outside the wall, twice as many families of the Chinese as there were of the Kitan. This regulation greatly increased the discontent of the Kitan, and made them more inclined to rebellion than they were before.

Besides this, there had been for some time a growing difficulty between the Chinese government and Genghis Khan. It seems that the Monguls had been for a long time accustomed to pay some sort of tribute to the Emperor of China, and many years before, while Genghis Khan, under the name of Temujin, was living at Karakorom, a subject of Vang Khan, the emperor sent a certain royal prince, named Yong-tsi, to receive what was due. While Yong-tsi was in the Mongul territory he and Temujin met, but they did not agree together at all. The Chinese prince put some slight upon Temujin, which Temujin resented. Very likely Temujin, whose character at that time, as well as afterward, was marked with a great deal of pride and spirit, opposed the payment of the tribute. At any rate, Yong-tsi became very much incensed against him, and, on his return, made serious charges against him to the emperor, and urged that he should be seized and put to death. But the emperor declined engaging in so dangerous an undertaking. Yong-tsi's proposal, however, became known to Temujin, and he secretly resolved that he would one day have his revenge.

At length, about three or four years after Temujin was raised to the throne, the emperor of the Chinese died, and Yong-tsi succeeded him. The very next year he sent an officer to Genghis Khan to demand the usual tribute. When the officer came into the presence of Genghis Khan in his camp, and made his demand, Genghis Khan asked him who was the emperor that had sent him with such a message.

The officer replied that Yong-tsi was at that time emperor of the Chinese.

"Yong-tsi!" repeated Genghis Khan, in a tone of great contempt. "The Chinese have a proverb," he added, "that such a people as they ought to have a god for their emperor; but it seems they do not know how to choose even a decent man."

It was true that they had such a proverb. They were as remarkable, it seems, in those days as they are now for their national self-importance and vanity.

"Go and tell your emperor," added Genghis Khan, "that I am a sovereign ruler, and that I will never acknowledge him as my master."

When the messenger returned with this defiant answer, Yong-tsi was very much enraged, and immediately began to prepare for war. Genghis Khan also at once commenced his preparations. He sent envoys to the leading khans who occupied the territories outside the wall inviting them to join him. He raised a great army, and put the several divisions of it under the charge of his ablest generals. Yong-tsi raised a great army too. The historians say that it amounted to three hundred thousand men. He put this army under the command of a great general named Hujaku, and ordered him to advance with it to the northward, so as to intercept the army of Genghis Khan on its way, and to defend the wall and the fortresses on the outside of it from his attacks.

In the campaign which ensued Genghis Khan was most successful. The Monguls took possession of a great many towns and fortresses beyond the wall, and every victory that they gained made the tribes and nations that inhabited those provinces more and more disposed to join them. Many of them revolted against the Chinese authority, and turned to their side. One of these was a chieftain so powerful that he commanded an army of one hundred thousand men. In order to bind himself solemnly to the covenant which he was to make with Genghis Khan, he ascended a mountain in company with the envoy and with others who were to witness the proceedings, and there performed the ceremony customary on such occasions. The ceremony consisted of sacrificing a white horse and a black ox, and then breaking an arrow, at the same time pronouncing an oath by which he bound himself under the most solemn sanctions to be faithful to Genghis Khan.

To reward the prince for this act of adhesion to his cause, Genghis Khan made him king over all that portion of the country, and caused him to be everywhere so proclaimed. This encouraged a great many other khans and chieftains to come over to his side; and at length one who had the command of one of the gates of the great wall, and of the fortress which defended it, joined him. By this means Genghis Khan obtained access to the interior of the Chinese dominions, and Yong-tsi and his great general Hujaku became seriously alarmed.

At length, after various marchings and counter-marchings, Genghis Khan learned that Hujaku was encamped with the whole of his army in a very strong position at the foot of a mountain, and he determined to proceed thither and attack him. He did so; and the result of the battle was that Hujaku was beaten and was forced to retreat. He retired to a great fortified town, and Genghis Khan followed him and laid siege to the town. Hujaku, finding himself in imminent danger, fled; and Genghis Khan was on the point of taking the town, when he was suddenly stopped in his career by being one day wounded severely by an arrow which was shot at him from the wall.

The wound was so severe that, while suffering under it, Genghis Khan found that he could not successfully direct the operations of his army, and so he withdrew his troops and retired into his own country, to wait there until his wound should be healed. In a few months he was entirely recovered, and the next year he fitted out a new expedition, and advanced again into China.

In the mean time, Hujaku, who had been repeatedly defeated and driven back the year before by Genghis Khan, had fallen into disgrace. His rivals and enemies among the other generals of the army, and among the officers of the court, conspired against him, and represented to the emperor that he was unfit to command, and that his having failed to defend the towns and the country that had been committed to him was owing to his cowardice and incapacity. In consequence of these representations Hujaku was cashiered, that is, dismissed from his command in disgrace.

This made him very angry, and he determined that he would have his revenge. There was a large party in his favor at court, as well as a party against him; and after a long and bitter contention, the former once more prevailed, and induced the emperor to restore Hujaku to his command again.

The quarrel, however, was not ended, and so, when Genghis Khan came the next year to renew the invasion, the councils of the Chinese were so distracted, and their operations so paralyzed by this feud, that he gained very easy victories over them. The Chinese generals, instead of acting together in a harmonious manner against the common enemy, were intent only on the quarrel which they were waging against each other.

At length the animosity proceeded to such an extreme that Hujaku resolved to depose the emperor, who seemed inclined rather to take part against him, assassinate all the chiefs of the opposite party, and then finally to put the emperor to death, and cause himself to be proclaimed in his stead.

In order to prepare the way for the execution of this scheme, he forbore to act vigorously against Genghis Khan and the Monguls, but allowed them to advance farther and farther into the country. This, of course, increased the general discontent and excitement, and prepared the way for the revolt which Hujaku was plotting.

At length the time for action arrived. Hujaku suddenly appeared at the head of a large force at the gates of the capital, and gave the alarm that the Monguls were coming. He pressed forward into the city to the palace, and gave the alarm there. At the same time, files of soldiers, whom he had ordered to this service, went to all parts of the city, arresting and putting to death all the leaders of the party opposed to him, under pretense that he had discovered a plot or conspiracy in which they were engaged to betray the city to the enemy. The excitement and confusion which was produced by this charge, and by the alarm occasioned by the supposed coming of the Monguls, so paralyzed the authorities of the town that nobody resisted Hujaku, or attempted to save the persons whom he arrested. Some of them he caused to be killed on the spot. Others he shut up in prison. Finding himself thus undisputed master of the city, he next took possession of the palace, seized the emperor, deposed him from his office, and shut him up in a dungeon. Soon afterward he put him to death.

This was the end of Yong-tsi; but Hujaku did not succeed, after all, in his design of causing himself to be proclaimed emperor in his stead. He found that there would be very great opposition to this, and so he gave up this part of his plan, and finally raised a certain prince of the royal family to the throne, while he retained his office of commander-in-chief of the forces. Having thus, as he thought, effectually destroyed the influence and power of his enemies at the capital, he put himself once more at the head of his troops, and went forth to meet Genghis Khan.

Some accident happened to him about this time by which his foot was hurt, so that he was, in some degree, disabled, but still he went on. At length he met the vanguard of Genghis Khan's army at a place where they were attempting to cross a river by a bridge. Hujaku determined immediately to attack them. The state of his foot was such that he could not walk nor even mount a horse, but he caused himself to be put upon a sort of car, and was by this means carried into the battle.

The Moguls were completely defeated and driven back. Perhaps this was because Genghis Khan was not there to command them. He was at some distance in the rear with the main body of the army.

Hujaku was very desirous of following up his victory by pursuing and attacking the Mogul vanguard the next day. He could not, however, do this personally, for, on account of the excitement and exposure which he had endured in the battle, and the rough movements and joltings which, notwithstanding all his care, he had to bear in being conveyed to and fro about the field, his foot grew much worse. Inflammation set in during the night, and the next day the wound opened afresh; so he was obliged to give up the idea of going out himself against the enemy, and to send one of his generals instead. The general to whom he gave the command was named Kan-ki.

Kan-ki went out against the enemy, but, after a time, returned unsuccessful. Hujaku was very angry with him when he came to hear his report. Perhaps the wound in his foot made him impatient and unreasonable. At any rate, he declared that the cause of Kan-ki's failure was his dilatoriness in pursuing the enemy, which was cowardice or treachery, and, in either case, he deserved to suffer death for it. He immediately sent to the emperor a report of the case, asking that the sentence of death which he had pronounced against Kan-ki might be confirmed, and that he might be authorized to put it into execution.

But the emperor, knowing that Kan-ki was a courageous and faithful officer, would not consent.

In the mean while, before the emperor's answer came back, the wrath of Hujaku had had time to cool a little. Accordingly, when he received the answer, he said to Kan-ki that he would, after all, try him once more.

"Take the command of the troops again," said he, "and go out against the enemy. If you beat them, I will overlook your first offense and spare your life; but if you are beaten yourself a second time, you shall die."

So Kan-ki placed himself at the head of his detachment, and went out again to attack the Monguls. They were to the northward, and were posted, it seems, upon or near a sandy plain. At any rate, a strong north wind began to blow at the time when the attack commenced, and blew the sand and dust into the eyes of his soldiers so that they could not see, while their enemies the Monguls, having their backs to the wind, were very little incommoded. The result was that Kan-ki was repulsed with considerable loss, and was obliged to make the best of his way back to Hujaku's quarters to save the remainder of his men.

He was now desperate. Hujaku had declared that if he came back without having gained a victory he should die, and he had no doubt that the man was violent and reckless enough to keep his word. He determined not to submit. He might as well die fighting, he thought, at the head of his troops, as to be ignobly put to death by Hujaku's executioner. So he arranged it with his troops, who probably hated Hujaku as much as he did, that, on returning to the town, they should march in under arms, take possession of the place, surround the palace, and seize the general and make him prisoner, or kill him if he should attempt any resistance.

The troops accordingly, when they arrived at the gates of the town, seized and disarmed the guards, and then marched in, brandishing their weapons, and uttering loud shouts and outcries, which excited first a feeling of astonishment and then of terror among the inhabitants. The alarm soon spread to the palace. Indeed, the troops themselves soon reached and surrounded the palace, and began thundering at the gates to gain admission. They soon forced their way in. Hujaku, in the mean time, terrified and panic-stricken, had fled from the palace into the gardens, in hopes to make his escape by the garden walls. The soldiers pursued him. In his excitement and agitation he leaped down from a wall too high for such a descent, and, in his fall, broke his leg. He lay writhing helplessly on the ground when the soldiers came up. They were wild and furious with the excitement of pursuit, and they killed him with their spears where he lay.

Kan-ki took the head of his old enemy and carried it to the capital, with the intention of offering it to the emperor, and also of surrendering himself to the officers of justice, in order, as he said, that he might be put to death for the crime of which he had been guilty in heading a military revolt and killing his superior officer. By all the laws of war this was a most heinous and a wholly unpardonable offense.

But the emperor was heartily glad that the turbulent and unmanageable old general was put out of the way, for a man so unprincipled, so ambitious, and so reckless as Hujaku was is always an object of aversion and terror to all who have anything to do with him. The emperor accordingly issued a proclamation, in which he declared that Hujaku had been justly put to death in punishment for many crimes which he had committed, and soon afterward he appointed Kan-ki commander-in-chief of the forces in his stead.

CHAPTER 16: CONQUESTS IN CHINA
1211-1216

War continued—Rich and fertile country—Grand invasion—Simultaneous attack by four armies—Enthusiasm of the troops—Captives—Immense plunder—Dreadful ravages—Base use made of the captives—Extent of Mongul conquests—The siege of Yen-king—Proposed terms of arrangement—Difference of opinion—Consultation on the subject—The conditions accepted—Terms of peace agreed upon—Consultations—The emperor's uneasiness—Abandonment of the capital—Revolt of the guards—The siege of the capital renewed—Wan-yen and Mon-yen—Their perplexity—Suicide proposed—Wan-yen in despair—His suicide—Mon-yen's plan—Petition of the wives—Sacking of the city by Mingan—Massacres—Fate of Mon-yen—Treasures—Conquests extended—Governors appointed.

After the death of Hujaku, the Emperor of China endeavored to defend his dominions against Genghis Khan by means of his other generals, and the war was continued for several years, during which time Genghis Khan made himself master of all the northern part of China, and ravaged the whole country in the most reckless and cruel manner. The country was very populous and very rich. The people, unlike the Monguls and Tartars, lived by tilling the ground, and they practiced, in great perfection, many manufacturing and mechanic arts. The country was very fertile, and, in the place of the boundless pasturages of the Mongul territories, it was covered in all directions with cultivated fields, gardens, orchards, and mulberry-groves, while thriving villages and busy towns were scattered over the whole face of it. It was to protect this busy hive of wealth and industry that the great wall had been built ages before; for the Chinese had always been stationary, industrious, and peaceful, while the territories of Central Asia, lying to the north of them, had been filled from time immemorial with wild, roaming, and unscrupulous troops of marauders, like those who were now united under the banner of Genghis Khan. The wall had afforded for some hundreds of years an adequate protection, for no commander had appeared of sufficient power to organize and combine the various hordes on a scale great enough to enable them to force so strong a barrier. But, now that Genghis Khan had come upon the stage, the barrier was broken through, and the terrible and reckless hordes poured in with all the force and fury of an inundation. In the year 1214, which was the year following that in which Hujaku was killed, Genghis Khan organized a force so large, for the invasion of China, that he divided it into four different battalions, which were to enter by different roads, and ravage different portions of the country. Each of these divisions was by itself a great and powerful army, and the simultaneous invasion of four such masses of reckless and merciless enemies filled the whole land with terror and dismay.

The Chinese emperor sent the best bodies of troops under his command to guard the passes in the mountains, and the bridges and fording-places on the rivers, hoping in this way to do something toward stemming the tide of these torrents of invasion. But it was all in vain. Genghis Khan had raised and equipped his forces by means, in a great measure, of the plunder which he had obtained in China the year before, and he had made great promises and glowing representations to his men in respect to the booty to be obtained in this new campaign. The troops were consequently full of ardor and enthusiasm, and they pressed on with such impetuosity as to carry all before them.

The Emperor of China, in pursuing his measures of defense, had ordered all the men capable of bearing arms in the villages and in the open country to repair to the nearest large city or fortress, there to be enrolled and equipped for service. The consequence was that the Monguls found in many places, as they advanced through the country, nobody but infirm old men, and women and children in the hamlets and villages. A great many of these, especially such as seemed to be of most consequence, the handsomest and best of the women, and the oldest children, they seized and took with them in continuing their march, intending to make slaves of them. They also took possession of all the gold and silver, and also of all the silks and other rich and valuable merchandise which they found, and distributed it as plunder. The spoil which they obtained, too, in sheep and cattle, was enormous. From it they made up immense flocks and herds, which were driven off into the Mongul country. The rest were slaughtered, and used to supply the army with food.

It was the custom of the invaders, after having pillaged a town and its environs, and taken away all which they could convert to any useful purpose for themselves, to burn the town itself, and then to march on, leaving in the place only a smoking heap of ruins, with the miserable remnant of the population which they had spared wandering about the scene of desolation in misery and despair.

They made a most cowardly and atrocious use, too, of the prisoners whom they conveyed away. When they arrived at a fortified town where there was a garrison or any other armed force prepared to resist them, they would bring forward these helpless captives, and put them in the fore-front of the battle in such a manner that the men on the walls could not shoot their arrows at their savage assailants without killing their own wives and children. The officers commanded the men to fire notwithstanding. But they were so moved by the piteous cries which the women and children made that they could not bear to do it, and so they refused to obey, and in the excitement and confusion thus produced the Monguls easily obtained possession of the town.

There are two great rivers in China, both of which flow from west to east, and they are at such a distance from each other and from the frontiers that they divide the territory into three nearly equal parts. The northernmost of these rivers is the Hoang Ho. The Monguls in the course of two years overran and made themselves masters of almost the whole country lying north of this river, that is, of about one third of China proper. There were, however, some strongly-fortified towns which they found it very difficult to conquer.

Among other places, there was the imperial city of Yen-king, where the emperor himself resided, which was so strongly defended that for some time the Monguls did not venture to attack it. At length, however, Genghis Khan came himself to the place, and concentrated there a very large force. The emperor and his court were very much alarmed, expecting an immediate assault. Still Genghis Khan hesitated. Some of his generals urged him to scale the walls, and so force his way into the city. But he thought it more politic to adopt a different plan.

So he sent an officer into the town with proposals of peace to be communicated to the emperor. In these proposals Genghis Khan said that he himself was inclined to spare the town, but that to appease his soldiers, who were furious to attack and pillage the city, it would be necessary to make them considerable presents, and that, if the emperor would agree to such terms with him as should enable him to satisfy his men in this respect, he would spare the city and would retire.

The emperor and his advisers were much perplexed at the receipt of this proposal. There was great difference of opinion among the counselors in respect to the reply which was to be made to it. Some were in favor of rejecting it at once. One general, not content with a simple rejection of it, proposed that, to show the indignation and resentment which they felt in receiving it, the garrison should march out of the gates and attack the Monguls in their camp.

There were other ministers, however, who urged the emperor to submit to the necessity of the case, and make peace with the conqueror. They said that the idea of going out to attack the enemy in their camp was too desperate to be entertained for a moment, and if they waited within the walls and attempted to defend themselves there, they exposed themselves to a terrible danger, without any countervailing hope of advantage at all commensurate with it; for if they failed to save the city they were all utterly and irretrievably ruined; and if, on the other hand, they succeeded in repelling the assault, it was only a brief respite that they could hope to gain, for the Monguls would soon return in greater numbers and in a higher state of excitement and fury than ever. Besides, they said, the garrison was discontented and depressed in spirit, and would make but a feeble resistance. It was composed mainly of troops brought in from the country, away from their families and homes, and all that they desired was to be released from duty, in order that they might go and see what had become of their wives and children.

The emperor, in the end, adopted this counsel, and he sent a commissioner to the camp of Genghis Khan to ask on what terms peace could be made. Genghis Khan stated the conditions. They were very hard, but the emperor was compelled to submit to them. One of the stipulations was that Genghis Khan was to receive one of the Chinese princesses, a daughter of the late emperor Yong-tsi, to add to the number of his wives. There were also to be delivered to him for slaves five hundred young boys and as many girls, three thousand horses, a large quantity of silk, and an immense sum of money. As soon as these conditions were fulfilled, after dividing the slaves and the booty among the officers and soldiers of his army, Genghis Khan raised the siege and moved off to the northward.

In respect to the captives that his soldiers had taken in the towns and villages—the women and children spoken of above—the army carried off with them all that were old enough to be of any value as slaves. The little children, who would only, they thought, be in the way, they massacred.

The emperor was by no means easy after the Mongul army had gone. A marauding enemy like that, bought off by the payment of a ransom, is exceedingly apt to find some pretext for returning, and the emperor did not feel that he was safe. Very soon after the Monguls had withdrawn, he proposed to his council the plan of removing his court southward to the other side of the Hoang Ho, to a large city in the province of Henan. Some of his counselors made great objections to this proposal. They said that if the emperor withdrew in that manner from the northern provinces that portion of his empire would be irretrievably lost. Genghis Khan would soon obtain complete and undisputed possession of the whole of it. The proper course to be adopted, they said, was to remain and make a firm stand in defense of the capital and of the country. They must levy new troops, repair the fortifications, recruit the garrison, and lay in supplies of food and of other military stores, and thus prepare themselves for a vigorous and efficient resistance in case the enemy should return.

But the emperor could not be persuaded. He said that the treasury was exhausted, the troops were discouraged, the cities around the capital were destroyed, and the whole country was so depopulated by the devastations of the

Monguls that no considerable number of fresh levies could be obtained; and that, consequently, the only safe course for the government to pursue was to retire to the southward, beyond the river. He would, however, he added, leave his son, with a strong garrison, to defend the capital.

He accordingly took with him a few favorites of his immediate family and a small body of troops, and commenced his journey—a journey which was considered by all the people as a base and ignoble flight. He involved himself in endless troubles by this step. A revolt broke out on the way among the guards who accompanied him. One of the generals who headed the revolt sent a messenger to Genghis Khan informing him of the emperor's abandonment of his capital, and offering to go over, with all the troops under his command, to the service of Genghis Khan if Genghis Khan would receive him.

When Genghis Khan heard thus of the retreat of the emperor from his capital, he was, or pretended to be, much incensed. He considered the proceeding as in some sense an act of hostility against himself, and, as such, an infraction of the treaty and a renewal of the war. So he immediately ordered one of his leading generals—a certain chieftain named Mingan—to proceed southward at the head of a large army and lay siege to Yen-king again.

The old emperor, who seems now to have lost all spirit, and to have given himself up entirely to despondency and fear, was greatly alarmed for the safety of his son the prince, whom he had left in command at Yen-king. He immediately sent orders to his son to leave the city and come to him. The departure of the prince, in obedience to these orders, of course threw an additional gloom over the city, and excited still more the general discontent which the emperor's conduct had awakened.

The prince, on his departure, left two generals in command of the garrison. Their names were Wan-yen and Mon-yen. They were left to defend the city as well as they could from the army of Monguls under Mingan, which was now rapidly drawing near. The generals were greatly embarrassed and perplexed with the difficulties of their situation. The means of defense at their disposal were wholly inadequate, and they knew not what to do.

At length one of them, Wan-yen, proposed to the other that they should kill themselves. This Mon-yen refused to do. Mon-yen was the commander on whom the troops chiefly relied, and he considered suicide a mode of deserting one's post scarcely less dishonorable than any other. He said that his duty was to stand by his troops, and, if he could not defend them where they were, to endeavor to draw them away, while there was an opportunity, to a place of safety.

So Wan-yen, finding his proposal rejected, went away in a rage. He retired to his apartment, and wrote a dispatch to the emperor, in which he explained the desperate condition of affairs, and the impossibility of saving the city, and in the end declared himself deserving of death for not being able to accomplish the work which his majesty had assigned to him.

He enveloped and sealed this dispatch, and then, calling his domestics together, he divided among them, in a very calm and composed manner, all his personal effects, and then took leave of them and dismissed them.

A single officer only now remained with him. In the presence of this officer he wrote a few words, and then sent him away. As soon as the officer had gone, he drank a cup of poison which he had previously ordered to be prepared for him, and in a few minutes was a lifeless corpse.

In the mean time, the other general, Mon-yen, had been making preparations to leave the city. His plan was to take with him such troops as might be serviceable to the emperor, but to leave all the inmates of the palace, as well as the inhabitants of the city, to their fate. Among the people of the palace were, it seems, a number of the emperor's wives, whom he had left behind at the time of his own flight, he having taken with him at that time only a few of the more favored ones. These women who were left, when they heard that Mon-yen was intending to abandon the city with a view of joining the emperor in the south, came to him in a body, and begged him to take them with him.

In order to relieve himself of their solicitations, he said that he would do so, but he added that he must leave the city himself with the guards to prepare the way, and that he would return immediately for them. They were satisfied with this promise, and returned to the palace to prepare for the journey. Mon-yen at once left the city, and very soon after he had gone, Mingan, the Mongul general, arrived at the gates, and, meeting with no effectual resistance, he easily forced his way in, and a scene of universal terror and confusion ensued. The soldiers spread themselves over the city in search of plunder, and killed all who came in their way. They plundered the palace and then set it on fire. So extensive was the edifice, and so vast were the stores of clothing and other valuables which it contained, even after all the treasures which could be made available to the conquerors had been taken away, that the fire continued to burn among the ruins for a month or more.

What became of the unhappy women who were so cruelly deceived by Mon-yen in respect to their hopes of escape does not directly appear. They doubtless perished with the other inhabitants of the city in the general massacre. Soldiers at such a time, while engaged in the sack and plunder of a city, are always excited to a species of insane fury, and take a savage delight in thrusting their pikes into all that come in their way.

Mon-yen excused himself, when he arrived at the quarters of the emperor, for having thus abandoned the women to their fate by the alleged impossibility of saving them. He could not have succeeded, he said, in effecting his own retreat and that of the troops who went with him if he had been encumbered in his movements by such a company of women. The emperor accepted this excuse, and seemed to be satisfied with it, though, not long afterward, Mon-yen was accused of conspiracy against the emperor and was put to death.

Mingan took possession of the imperial treasury, where he found great stores of silk, and also of gold and silver plate. All these things he sent to Genghis Khan, who remained still at the north at a grand encampment which he had made in Tartary.

After this, other campaigns were fought by Genghis Khan in China, in the course of which he extended his conquests still farther to the southward, and made himself master of a very great extent of country. After confirming these conquests, he selected from among such Chinese officers as were disposed to enter into his service suitable persons to be appointed governors of the provinces, and in this way annexed them to his dominions; these officers thus transferring their allegiance from the emperor to him, and covenanting to send to him the tribute which they should annually collect from their respective dominions. Everything being thus settled in this quarter, Genghis Khan next turned his attention to the western frontiers of his empire, where the Tartar and Mongul territory bordered on Turkestan and the dominions of the Mohammedans.

CHAPTER 17: THE SULTAN MOHAMMED
1217

Mohammedan countries on the west—Sultan Mohammed—Karazm—Proposed embassy—Makinut and his suite—Speech of the ambassador—Father and son— The sultan not pleased—Private interview—Anger of the sultan—Conversation— Makinut returns a soft answer—The sultan is appeased—Treaty made—Genghis Khan is pleased—Opening of the trade—The exorbitant merchants—Their punishment—The next company—Their artful management—Genghis Khan fits out a company—Ambassadors—Mohammedans—Messengers from the court— Large party—Roads doubly guarded—The Calif of Bagdad—Mohammed's demand and the calif's reply—The sultan calls a council—Mohammed's plan for revenge—March of the army—Failure—The calif's plans—Objections to them— Arguments of the calif—Message to Genghis Khan—Artful device—The answer of Genghis Khan—The caravan arrives at Otrar—The governor's treachery—The party massacred—Genghis Khan hears the tidings—He declares war— Preparations.

The portion of China which Genghis Khan had added to his dominions by the conquests described in the last chapter was called Katay, and the possession of it, added to the extensive territories which were previously under his sway, made his empire very vast. The country which he now held, either under his direct government, or as tributary provinces and kingdoms, extended north and south through the whole interior of Asia, and from the shores of the Japan and China Seas on the east, nearly to the Caspian Sea on the west, a distance of nearly three thousand miles.

Beyond his western limits lay Turkestan and other countries governed by the Mohammedans. Among the other Mohammedan princes there was a certain Sultan Mohammed, a great and very powerful sovereign, who reigned over an extensive region in the neighborhood of the Caspian Sea, though the principal seat of his power was a country called Karazm. He was, in consequence, sometimes styled Mohammed Karazm.

It might perhaps have been expected that Genghis Khan, having subdued all the rivals within his reach in the eastern part of Asia, and being strong and secure in the possession of his power, would have found some pretext for making war upon the sultan, with a view of conquering his territories too, and adding the countries bordering on the Caspian to his dominions. But, for some reason or other, he concluded, in this instance, to adopt a different policy. Whether it was that he was tired of war and wished for repose, or whether the sultan's dominions were too remote, or his power too great to make it prudent to attack him, he determined on sending an embassy instead of an army, with a view of proposing to the sultan a treaty of friendship and alliance.

The time when this embassy was sent was in the year 1217, and the name of the principal ambassador was Makinut.

Makinut set out on his mission accompanied by a large retinue of attendants and guards. The journey occupied several weeks, but at length he arrived in the sultan's dominions. Soon after his arrival he was admitted to an audience of the sultan, and there, accompanied by his own secretaries, and in the presence of all the chief officers of the sultan's court, he delivered his message.

He gave an account in his speech of the recent victories which his sovereign, Genghis Khan, had won, and of the great extension which his empire had in consequence attained. He was now become master, he said, of all the countries of Central Asia, from the eastern extremity of the continent up to the frontiers of the sultan's dominions, and having thus become the sultan's neighbor, he was desirous of entering into a treaty of amity and alliance with him, which would be obviously for the mutual interest of both. He had accordingly been sent an ambassador to the sultan's court to propose such an alliance. In offering it, the emperor, he said, was actuated by a feeling of the sincerest good-will. He wished the sultan to consider him as a father, and he would look upon the sultan as a son.

According to the patriarchal ideas of government which prevailed in those days, the relation of father to son involved not merely the idea of a tie of affection connecting an older with a younger person, but it implied something of pre-eminence and authority on the one part, and dependence and subjection on the other. Perhaps Genghis Khan did not mean his proposition to be understood in this sense, but made it solely in reference to the disparity between his own and the sultan's years, for he was himself now becoming considerably advanced in life. However this may be, the sultan was at first not at all pleased with the proposition in the form in which the ambassador made it.

He, however, listened quietly to Makinut's words, and said nothing until the public audience was ended. He then took Makinut alone into another apartment in order to have some quiet conversation with him. He first asked him to tell him the exact state of the case in respect to all the pretended victories which Genghis Khan had gained, and, in order to propitiate him and induce him to reveal the honest truth, he made him a present of a rich scarf, splendidly adorned with jewels.

"How is it?" said he; "has the emperor really made all those conquests, and is his empire as extensive and powerful as he pretends? Tell me the honest truth about it."

"What I have told your majesty is the honest truth about it," replied Makinut. "My master the emperor is as powerful as I have represented him, and this your majesty will soon find out in case you come to have any difficulty with him."

This bold and defiant language on the part of the ambassador greatly increased the irritation which the sultan felt before. He seemed much incensed, and replied in a very angry manner.

"I know not what your master means," said he, "by sending such messages to me, telling me of the provinces that he has conquered, and boasting of his power, or upon what ground he pretends to be greater than I, and expects that I shall honor him as my father, and be content to be treated by him only as his son. Is he so very great a personage as this?"

Makinut now found that perhaps he had spoken a little too plainly, and he began immediately to soften and modify what he had said, and to compliment the sultan himself, who, as he was well aware, was really superior in power and glory to Genghis Khan, notwithstanding the great extension to which the empire of the latter had recently attained. He also begged that the sultan would not be angry with him for delivering the message with which he had been intrusted. He was only a servant, he said, and he was bound to obey the orders of his master. He assured the sultan, moreover, that if any unfavorable construction could by possibility be put upon the language which the emperor had used, no such meaning was designed on his part, but that in sending the embassage, and in everything connected with it, the emperor had acted with the most friendly and honorable intentions.

By means of conciliating language like this the sultan was at length appeased, and he finally was induced to agree to everything which the ambassador proposed. A treaty of peace and commerce was drawn up and signed, and, after everything was concluded, Makinut returned to the Mongul country loaded with presents, some of which were for himself and his attendants, and others were for Genghis Khan.

He was accompanied, too, by a caravan of merchants, who, in consequence of the new treaty, were going into the country of Genghis Khan with their goods, to see what they could do in the new market thus opened to them. This caravan traveled in company with Makinut on his return, in order to avail themselves of the protection which the guard that attended him could afford in passing through the intervening countries. These countries being filled with hordes of Tartars, who were very little under the dominion of law, it would have been unsafe for a caravan of rich merchandise to pass through them without an escort.

Genghis Khan was greatly pleased with the result of his embassy. He was also much gratified with the presents that the sultan had sent him, which consisted of costly stuffs for garments, beautiful and highly-wrought arms, precious stones, and other similar articles. He welcomed the merchants too, and opened facilities for them to travel freely throughout his dominions and dispose of their goods.

In order that future caravans might go and come at all times in safety, he established guards along the roads between his country and that of the sultan. These guards occupied fortresses built at convenient places along the way, and especially at the crossing-places on the rivers, and in the passes of the mountains; and there orders were given to these guards to scour the country in every direction around their respective posts, in order to keep it clear of robbers. Whenever a band of robbers was formed, the soldiers hunted them from one lurking-place to another until they were exterminated. In this way, after a short time, the country became perfectly safe, and the caravans of merchants could go and come with the richest goods, and even with treasures of gold and silver, without any fear.

At first, it would seem, some of the merchants from the countries of Mohammed asked too much for their goods. At least a story is told of a company who came very soon after the opening of the treaty, and who offered their goods first to Genghis Khan himself, but they asked such high prices for them that he was astonished.

"I suppose," said he, "by your asking such prices as these, you imagine that I have never bought any goods before."

He then took them to see his treasures, and showed them over a thousand large chests filled with valuables of every description; gold and silver utensils, rich silks, arms and accoutrements splendidly adorned with precious stones, and other such commodities. He told them that he showed them these things in order that they might see that he had had some experience in respect to dealings in merchandise of that sort before, and knew something of its just value. And that, since they had been so exorbitant in their demands, presuming probably upon the ignorance of those whom they came to deal with, he should send them back with all their goods, and not allow them to sell them anywhere in his dominions, at any price.

MERCHANTS OFFERING THEIR GOODS.

This threat he put in execution. The merchants were obliged to go back without selling any of their goods at all.

The next company of merchants that came, having heard of the adventure of the others, determined to act on a different principle. Accordingly, when they came into the presence of the khan with their goods, and he asked them the prices of some of them, they replied that his majesty might himself fix the price of the articles, as he was a far better judge of the value of such things than they were. Indeed, they added that if his majesty chose to take them without paying any thing at all he was welcome to do so.

This answer pleased the emperor very much. He paid them double price for the articles which he selected from their stores, and he granted them peculiar privileges in respect to trading with his subjects while they remained in his dominions.

The trade which was thus opened between the dominions of the sultan and those of Genghis Khan was not, however, wholly in the hands of merchants coming from the former country. Soon after the coming of the caravan last mentioned, Genghis Khan fitted out a company of merchants from his own country, who were to go into the country of the sultan, taking with them such articles, the products of the country of the Monguls, as they might hope to find a

105

market for there. There were four principal merchants, but they were attended by a great number of assistants, servants, camel-drivers, etc., so that the whole company formed quite a large caravan. Genghis Khan sent with them three ambassadors, who were to present to the sultan renewed assurances of the friendly feelings which he entertained for him, and of his desire to encourage and promote as much as possible the commercial intercourse between the two countries which had been so happily begun.

The three ambassadors whom Genghis Khan selected for this service were themselves Mohammedans. He had several persons of this faith among the officers of his court, although the Monguls had a national religion of their own, which was very different from that of the Mohammedans; still, all forms of worship were tolerated in Genghis Khan's dominions, and the emperor was accustomed to take good officers into his service wherever he could find them, without paying any regard to the nature of their religious belief so far as their general duties were concerned. But now, in sending this deputation to the sultan, he selected the ambassadors from among the Mohammedans at his court, thinking that it would please the sultan better to receive his message through persons of his own religious faith. Besides, the three persons whom he appointed were natives of Turkestan, and they were, of course, well acquainted with the language of the country and with the country itself.

Besides the merchants and the ambassadors, Genghis Khan gave permission to each of his wives, and also to each of the great lords of his court, to send a servant or messenger with the caravan, to select and purchase for their masters and mistresses whatever they might find most curious or useful in the Mohammedan cities which the caravan might visit. The lords and ladies were all very glad to avail themselves of the opportunity thus afforded them.

All these persons, the ambassadors and their suite, the merchants and their servants, and the special messengers sent by the lords and ladies of the court, formed, as may well be supposed, a very numerous company. It is said that the caravan, when ready to commence its march, contained no less than four hundred and fifty persons.

Everything being at last made ready, the caravan set out on its long journey. It was accompanied by a suitable escort, and, in order to provide still more effectually for the safety of the rich merchandise and the valuable lives committed to it, Genghis Khan sent on orders beforehand to all the military stations on the way, directing the captains to double the guard on their respective sections of the road while the caravan was passing.

By means of these and other similar precautions the expedition accomplished the journey in safety, and arrived without any misfortune in the Mohammedan country. Very serious misfortunes, however, awaited them there immediately after their arrival, arising out of a train of events which had been for some time in progress, and which I must now go back a little to describe.

It seems that some difference had arisen some time before this between the Sultan Mohammed and the Calif of Bagdad, who was the great head of the Mohammedan power. Mohammed applied to the calif to grant him certain privileges and powers which had occasionally been bestowed on other sultans who had rendered great services to the Mohammedan empire. He claimed that he had merited these rewards by the services which he had rendered. He had conquered, he said, more than one hundred princes and chieftains, and had cut off their heads and annexed their territories to his dominions, thus greatly enlarging and extending the Mohammedan power.

Mohammed made this demand of the calif through the medium of an ambassador whom he sent to Bagdad. The calif, after hearing what the ambassador had to say, refused to comply. He said that the services which Mohammed had rendered were not of sufficient importance and value to merit the honors and privileges which Mohammed demanded. But, although he thus declined complying with Mohammed's request, he showed a disposition to treat the sultan himself with all proper deference by sending an ambassador of his own to accompany Mohammed's ambassador on his return, with instructions to communicate the reply which the calif felt bound to make in a respectful and courteous manner.

Mohammed received the calif's ambassador very honorably, and in his presence concealed the anger which the answer of the calif excited in his mind. As soon as the ambassador was gone, however, he convened a grand council of all the great chieftains, and generals, and ministers of state in his dominions, and announced to them his determination to raise an army and march to Bagdad, with a view of deposing the calif and reigning in his stead. The great personages assembled at the council were very ready to enter into this scheme, for they knew that if it was successful there would be a great many honors and a great deal of booty that would fall to their share in the final distribution of the spoil. So they all engaged with great zeal in aiding the sultan to form and equip his army. In due time the expedition was ready, and the sultan commenced his march. But, as often happens in such cases, the preparations had been hindered by various causes of delay, and it was too late in the season when the army began to move. The forces moved slowly, too, after they commenced their march, so that the winter came on while they were among the passes of the mountains. The winter was unusually severe, and the troops suffered so much from the frosts and the rains, and from the various hardships to which they were in consequence exposed, that the sultan found it impossible to go on. He was consequently obliged to return, and begin his work over again. And the worst of it was, that the calif was now aware of his designs, and would be able, he knew, before the next season, to take effectual measures to defend himself.

When the calif heard of the misfortunes which had befallen the sultan's army, and his narrow escape from the dangers of a formidable invasion, he was at first overjoyed, and he resolved at once on making war upon the rebellious sultan. In forming his plans for the campaign, the idea occurred to him of endeavoring to incite Genghis Khan to invade the sultan's dominions from the east while he himself attacked him from the west; for Bagdad, the capital of the calif, was to the westward of the sultan's country, as the empire of the Monguls was to the eastward of it.

But when the calif proposed his plan to his counselors, some of them objected to it very strenuously. The sultan and the people of his country were, like the calif himself, Mohammedans, while the Monguls were of another religion altogether, or, as the Mohammedans called them, unbelievers or infidels; and the counselors who objected to the calif's proposal said that it would be very wrong to bring the enemies of God into the country of the faithful to guard against a present and temporary danger, and thereby, perhaps, in the end occasion the ruin both of their religion and their empire. It would be an impious deed, they thought, thus to bring in a horde of barbarian infidels to wage war with them against their brethren.

To this the calif replied that the emergency was so critical that they were justified in availing themselves of any means that offered to save themselves from the ruin with which they were threatened. And as to the possibility that Genghis Khan, if admitted to the country as their ally, would in the end turn his arms against them, he said that they must watch, and take measures to guard against such a danger. Besides, he would rather have an open unbeliever like Genghis Khan for a foe, than a Mohammedan traitor and rebel like the sultan. He added, moreover, that he did not believe that the Mongul emperor felt any animosity or ill will against the Mohammedans or against their faith. It was evident, indeed, that he did not, for he had a great many Mohammedans in his dominions, and he allowed them to live there without molestation. He even had Mohammedan officers of very high rank in his court.

So it was finally decided to send a message and invite him to join the calif in making war on the sultan.

The difficulty was now to contrive some means by which this message could be conveyed through the sultan's territories, which, of course, lay between the dominions of the calif and those of Genghis Khan. To accomplish this purpose the calif resorted to a very singular device. Instead of writing his communication in a letter, he caused it to be pricked with a needle and some indigo, by a sort of tattooing process, upon the messenger's head, in such a manner that it was concealed by his hair. The messenger was then disguised as a countryman and sent forth. He succeeded in accomplishing the journey in safety, and when he arrived Genghis Khan had only to cause his head to be shaved, when the inscription containing the calif's proposal to him at once became legible.

This method of making the communication was considered very safe, for even if, from any accident, the man had been intercepted on the way, on suspicion of his being a messenger, the sultan's men would have found nothing, in searching him, to confirm their suspicions, for it is not at all probable that they would have thought of looking for a letter among his hair.

Genghis Khan was well pleased to receive the proposals of the calif, but he sent back word in reply that he could not at present engage in any hostile movement against the sultan on account of the treaty of peace and commerce which he had recently established with him. So long as the sultan observed the stipulations of the treaty, he felt bound in honor, he said, not to break it. He knew, however, he added, that the restless spirit of the sultan would not long allow things to remain in the posture they were then in, and that on the first occasion given he would not fail to declare war against him.

Things were in this state when the grand caravan of merchants and ambassadors which Genghis Khan had sent arrived at the frontiers of the sultan's dominions.

After passing the frontier, the first important place which they reached was a city called Otrar. They were received very courteously by the governor of this place, and were much pleased with the opportunity afforded them to rest from the fatigues of their long journey. It seems, however, after all, that the governor's friendship for his guests was only pretended, for he immediately wrote to the sultan, informing him that a party of persons had arrived at his city from the Mongul country who pretended to be merchants and ambassadors, but that he believed that they were spies, for they were extremely inquisitive about the strength of the garrisons and the state of the defenses of the country generally. He had no doubt, he added, that they were emissaries sent by Genghis Khan to find out the best way of invading his dominions.

One account states that the motive which induced the governor to make these representations to the sultan was some offense which he took at the familiar manner in which he was addressed by one of the ambassadors, who was a native of Otrar, and had known the governor in former times when he was a private person. Another says that his object was to have the expedition broken up, in order that he might seize for himself the rich merchandise and the valuable presents which the merchants and ambassadors had in their possession.

At any rate, he wrote to the sultan denouncing the whole party as foreign emissaries and spies, and in a short time he received a reply from the sultan directing him to put them all to death, or otherwise to deal with them as he thought proper. So he invited the whole party to a grand entertainment in his palace, and then, at a given signal, probably after most of them had become in some measure helpless from the influence of the wine, a body of his guards rushed in and massacred them all.

Or, rather, they attempted to massacre them all, but one of the merchants' men contrived in the confusion to make his escape. He succeeded in getting back into the Mongul country, where he reported what had happened to Genghis Khan.

Genghis Khan was greatly exasperated when he heard these tidings. He immediately called together his sons, and all the great lords and chieftains of his court, and recited to them the story of the massacre of the merchants in such a manner as to fill their hearts with indignation and rage, and to inspire them all with a burning thirst for revenge.

He also immediately sent word to the sultan that, since by so infamous an action he had violated all the engagements which had subsisted between them, he, from that instant, declared himself his mortal enemy, and would take vengeance upon him for his treacherousness and cruelty by ravaging his country with fire and sword.

This message was sent, it was said, by three ambassadors, whose persons ought to have been considered sacred, according to every principle of international law. But the sultan, as soon as they had delivered their message, ordered their heads to be cut off.

This new massacre excited the rage and fury of Genghis Khan to a higher pitch than ever. For three days, it is said, he neither ate nor slept, and seemed almost beside himself with mingled vexation, grief, and anger. And afterward he busied himself night and day with the arrangements for assembling his army and preparing to march, and he allowed himself no rest until everything was ready.

CHAPTER 18: THE WAR WITH THE SULTAN
1217-1218

Marshaling of the army—Arms and armor—Provision for contingencies—The army commences its march—Jughi's division—Preparations of the sultan—His army—His plan—The sultan meets Jughi—Opinion of the generals—Jughi's decision—The battle commenced—Neither party victorious—Jughi withdraws—His reception by his father—The Monguls victorious—The sultan's plans—Flying squadron—Genghis Khan.

Genghis Khan made his preparations for a war on an immense scale. He sent messengers in every direction to all the princes, khans, governors, and other chieftains throughout his empire, with letters explaining to them the cause of the war, and ordering them to repair to the places of rendezvous which he appointed, with all the troops that they could raise.

He gave particular directions in respect to the manner in which the men were to be armed and equipped. The arms required were the sabre, the bow, with a quiver full of arrows, and the battle-axe. Each soldier was also to carry a rope, ropes and cordage being continually in demand among people living on horseback and in tents.

The officers were to wear armor as well as to carry arms. Those who could afford it were to provide themselves with a complete coat of mail. The rest were to wear helmets and breast-plates only. The horses were also to be protected as far as possible by breast-plates, either of iron, or of leather thick and tough enough to prevent an arrow from penetrating.

When the troops thus called for appeared at the place of rendezvous appointed for them, Genghis Khan found, as is said, that he had an army of seven hundred thousand men!

The army being thus assembled, Genghis Khan caused certain rules and regulations, or articles of war, as they might be called, to be drawn up and promulgated to the troops. One of the rules was that no body of troops were ever to retreat without first fighting, whatever the imminence of the danger might be. He also ordered that where a body of men were engaged, if any subordinate division of them, as one company in a regiment, or one regiment in a battalion, should break ranks and fly before the order for a retreat should have been given by the proper authority, the rest were to leave fighting the enemy, and attack the portion flying, and kill them all upon the spot.

The emperor also made formal provision for the event of his dying in the course of the campaign. In this case a grand assembly of all the khans and chieftains of the empire was to be convened, and then, in the presence of these khans and of his sons, the constitution and laws of the empire, as he had established them, were to be read, and after the reading the assembly were to proceed to the election of a new khan, according to the forms which the constitution had provided.

After all these affairs had been arranged, Genghis Khan put his army in motion. He was obliged, of course, to separate it into several grand divisions, and to send the several divisions forward by different roads, and through different sections of the country. So large a body can never be kept together on a long march, on account of the immense quantity of food that is required, both for the horses and the men, and which must be supplied in the main by the country itself which they traverse, since neither horses nor men can carry food with them for more than a very few days.

Genghis Khan put one of the largest divisions under the command of his son Jughi, the prince who distinguished himself so much in the conflicts by which his father raised himself to the supreme power.

Jughi was ordered to advance with his division through Turkestan, the country where the Prince Kushluk had sought refuge, and which still remained, in some degree, disaffected toward Genghis Khan. Genghis Khan himself, with the main body of the army, took a more southerly route directly toward the dominions of the sultan.

In the mean time the sultan himself had not been idle. He collected together all the forces that he could command. When they were mustered, the number of men was found to be four hundred thousand. This was a large army, though much smaller than that of Genghis Khan.

The sultan set out upon his march with his troops to meet the invaders. After advancing for some distance, he learned that the army of Jughi, which had passed through Turkestan, was at the northward of his position, and he found that by turning in that direction he might hope to meet and conquer that part of the Mongul force before it could have time to join the main body. He determined at once to adopt this plan.

He accordingly turned his course, and marched forward into the part of the country where he supposed Jughi to be. At length he came to a place where his scouts found, near a river, a great many dead bodies lying on the ground. Among the others who had fallen there was one man who was wounded, but was not dead. This wounded man told the scouts that the bodies were those of persons who had been slain by the army of Jughi, which had just passed that way. The sultan accordingly pressed forward and soon overtook them. Jughi was hastening on in order to join his father.

Jughi consulted his generals in respect to what it was best to do. They advised him to avoid a battle.

"We are not strong enough," said they, "to encounter alone the whole of the sultan's army. It is better that we should retreat, which we can do in an orderly manner, and thus join the main body before we give the enemy battle. Or, if the sultan should attempt to pursue us, he cannot keep his army together in doing so. They will necessarily become divided into detachments on the road, and then we can turn and destroy them in detail, which will be a much surer mode of proceeding than for us to attack them in the mass."

Jughi was not willing to follow this advice.

"What will my father and my brothers think," said he, "when they see us coming to them, flying from the enemy, without having fought them, contrary to his express commands? No. We must stand our ground, trusting to our valor, and do our best. If we are to die at all, we had better be slain in battle than in flight. You have done your duty in admonishing me of the danger we are in, and now it remains for me to do mine in trying to bring you out of it with honor."

So he ordered the army to halt, and to be drawn up in order of battle.

The battle was soon commenced, and it was continued throughout the day. The Monguls, though fewer in numbers, were superior to their enemies in discipline and in courage, and the advantage was obviously on their side, though they did not gain a decisive victory. Toward night, however, the sultan's troops evinced every where a disposition to give way, and it was with great difficulty that the officers could induce them to maintain their ground until the darkness came on and put an end to the conflict. When at length the combatants could no longer see to distinguish friend from foe, the two armies withdrew to their respective camps, and built their fires for the night.

Jughi thought that by fighting during this day he had done all that his father required of him to vindicate the honor of the army, and that now it would be most prudent to retreat, without risking another battle on the morrow. So he caused fresh supplies of fuel to be put upon the camp-fires in order to deceive the enemy, and then marched out of his camp in the night with all his men. The next morning, by the time that the sultan's troops were again under arms, he had advanced far on his march to join his father, and was beyond their reach.

He soon rejoined his father, and was received by him with great joy. Genghis Khan was extremely pleased with the course which his son had pursued, and bestowed upon him many public honors and rewards.

After this other great battles were fought between the two armies. At one of them, a great trumpet fifteen feet long is mentioned among the other martial instruments that were used to excite the men to ardor in making the charge.

In these battles the Monguls were victorious. The sultan, however, still continued to make head as well as he could against the invaders, until at length he found that he had lost one hundred and sixty thousand of his men. This was almost half of his army, and the loss enfeebled him so much that he was convinced that it was useless for him any longer to resist the Monguls in the open field; so he sent off his army in detachments to the different towns and fortresses of his kingdom, ordering the several divisions to shut themselves up and defend themselves as well as they could, in the places assigned to them, until better times should return.

The sultan, however, did not seek shelter in this way for himself. He selected from his troops a certain portion of those who were most active and alert and were best mounted, and formed of them a sort of flying squadron with which he could move rapidly from place to place through the country, wherever his aid might be most required.

Genghis Khan, of course, now prepared to attack the cities where the several divisions of the sultan's army had intrenched themselves. He wished first to get possession of Otrar, which was the place where the ambassadors and the merchants had been massacred. But the city was not very large, and so, instead of marching toward it himself, he gave the charge of capturing it to two of his younger sons, whom he sent off for the purpose at the head of a suitable detachment.

He himself, with the main body, set off upon a march toward the cities of Samarcand and Bokhara, which were the great central cities of the sultan's dominions.

CHAPTER 19: THE FALL OF BOKHARA
1218-1219

Description of the town Bokhara—Zarnuk—An immediate surrender—Nur—Fate of Nur—The siege of Bokhara commenced—The sultan's anxiety—Intercepted letters—The deserter—The outer wall taken—Grand sortie made by the garrison—Evacuation of the town—Pursuit—The fugitives overtaken—Surrender—Conditions made—The governor of the citadel—Genghis Khan enters the city—Valuables surrendered—The emperor in the mosque—Desecration of the mosque—Genghis Khan makes a speech—The inhabitants give up everything—Conflagration—Surrender of the citadel—The town utterly destroyed—News of the fall of Otrar—Plans for the defense of Otrar—Sorties—The proposal made to Genghis Khan—The siege renewed—The outer walls taken—Desperate conflicts—Kariakas and the governor—Treason—Punishment of treason—The Monguls enter the town—Citadel stormed—Desperation of the governor—Courage and devotion of his wife—The governor's fate.

Bokhara was a great and beautiful city. It was situated in the midst of a very fine and fertile country, in a position very favorable for the trade and commerce of those days. It was also a great seat of learning and of the arts and sciences. It contained many institutions in which were taught such arts and sciences as were then cultivated, and students resorted to it from all the portions of Western Asia.

The city proper was inclosed with a strong wall. Besides this there was an outer wall, thirty miles in circumference, which inclosed the suburbs of the town, and also a beautiful region of parks and gardens, which contained the public places of amusement and the villas of the wealthy inhabitants. It was this peaceful seat of industry and wealth that Genghis Khan, with his hordes of ruthless barbarians, was coming now to sack and plunder.

The first city which the Monguls reached on their march toward Bokhara was one named Zarnuk. In approaching it a large troop rode up toward the walls, uttering terrific shouts and outcries. The people shut the gates in great terror. Genghis Khan, however, sent an officer to them to say that it was useless for them to attempt to resist him, and to advise them to surrender at once. They must demolish their citadel, he said, and send out all the young and able-bodied men to Genghis Khan. The officer advised them, too, to send out presents to Genghis Khan as an additional means of propitiating him and inducing him to spare the town.

The inhabitants yielded to this advice. The gates were thrown open. All the young men who were capable of bearing arms were marshaled and marched out to the Mongul camp. They were accompanied by the older men among the inhabitants, who took with them the best that the town contained, for presents. Genghis Khan accepted the presents, ordered the young men to be enrolled in his army, and then, dismissing the older ones in peace, he resumed his march and went on his way.

He next came to a town named Nur. One of the men from Zarnuk served as a guide to show the detachment which was sent to summon the city a near way to reach it. Nur was a sort of sacred town, having many holy places in it which were resorted to by many pilgrims and other devotees.

The people of Nur shut the gates and for some time refused to surrender. But at last, finding that it was useless to attempt to resist, they opened the gates and allowed the Monguls to come in. Genghis Khan, to punish the inhabitants, as he said, for even thinking of resisting him, set aside a supply of cattle and other provisions to keep them from starving, and then gave up all the rest of the property found in the town to be divided among his soldiers as plunder.

At length the army reached the great plain in which Bokhara was situated, and encamped before the town. Bokhara was very large and very populous, as may well be supposed from its outer wall of thirty miles in circuit, and Genghis Khan did not expect to make himself master of it without considerable difficulty and delay. He was, however, very intent on besieging and taking it, not only on account of the general wealth and importance of the place, but also because he supposed that the sultan himself was at this time within the walls. He had heard that the sultan had retreated there with his flying squadron, taking with him all his treasure.

This was, however, a mistake. The sultan was not there. He had gone there, it is true, at first, and had taken with him the most valuable of his treasures, but before Genghis Khan arrived he had secretly withdrawn to Samarcand, thinking that he might be safer there.

In truth, the sultan was beginning to be very much disheartened and discouraged. Among other things which occurred to disturb his mind, certain letters were found and brought to him, as if they had been intercepted, which letters gave accounts of a conspiracy among his officers to desert him and go over to the side of Genghis Khan. These letters were not signed, and the sultan could not discover who had written them, but the pretended conspiracy which they revealed filled his soul with anxiety and distress.

It was only a pretended conspiracy after all, for the letters were written by a man in Genghis Khan's camp, and with Genghis Khan's permission or connivance. This man was a Mohammedan, and had been in the sultan's service; but the sultan had put to death his father and his brothers on account of some alleged offense, and he had become so incensed at the act that he had deserted to Genghis Khan, and now he was determined to do his former sovereign all the mischief in his power. His intimate knowledge of persons and things connected with the sultan's court and army enabled him to write these letters in such a way as to deceive the sultan completely.

It was past midsummer when the army of Genghis Khan laid siege to Bokhara, and it was not until the spring of the following year that they succeeded in carrying the outer wall, so strongly was the city fortified and so well was it defended. After having forced the outer wall, the Monguls destroyed the suburbs of the town, devastated the cultivated gardens and grounds, and pillaged the villas. They then took up their position around the inner wall, and commenced the siege of the city itself in due form.

The sultan had left three of his greatest generals in command of the town. These men determined not to wait the operations of Genghis Khan in attacking the walls, but to make a sudden sally from the gates, with the whole force that could be spared, and attack the besiegers in their intrenchments. They made this sally in the night, at a time when the Monguls were least expecting it. They were, however, wholly unsuccessful. They were driven back into the city with great loss. The generals, it seems, had determined to risk all on this desperate attempt, and, in case it failed, at once to abandon the city to its fate. Accordingly, when driven into the city through the gates on one side, they marched directly through it and passed out through the gates on the other side, hoping to save themselves and the garrison by this retreat, with a view of ultimately rejoining the sultan. They, however, went first in a southerly direction from the city toward the River Amoor. The generals took their families and those of the principal officers of the garrison with them.

The night was dark, and they succeeded in leaving the city without being observed. In the morning, however, all was discovered, and Genghis Khan sent off a strong detachment of well-mounted troops in pursuit. These troops, after about a day's chase, overtook the flying garrison near the river. There was no escape for the poor fugitives, and the merciless Monguls destroyed them almost every one by riding over them, trampling them down with their horses' hoofs, and cutting them to pieces with their sabres.

In the mean time, while this detachment had been pursuing the garrison, Genghis Khan, knowing that there were no longer any troops within the city to defend it, and that everything there was in utter confusion, determined on a grand final assault; but, while his men were getting the engines ready to batter down the walls, a procession, consisting of all the magistrates and clergy, and a great mass of the principal citizens, came forth from one of the gates, bearing with them the keys of the city. These keys they offered to Genghis Khan in token of surrender, and begged him to spare their lives.

The emperor received the keys, and said to the citizens that he would spare their lives on condition that, if there were any of the sultan's soldiers concealed in the city, they would give them up, and that they would also seize and deliver to him any of the citizens that were suspected of being in the sultan's interest. This they took a solemn oath that they would do.

The soldiers, however—that is, those that remained in the town—were not delivered up. Most of them retired to the castle, which was a sort of citadel, and put themselves under the command of the governor of the castle, who, being a very energetic and resolute man, declared that he never would surrender.

There were a great many of the young men of the town, sons of the leading citizens, who also retired to the castle, determined not to yield to the conqueror.

Genghis Khan, having thus obtained the keys of the city itself, caused the gates to be opened, and his troops marched in and took possession. He had promised the citizens that his soldiers should spare the lives of the people and should not pillage the houses on condition that the magistrates delivered up peaceably the public magazines of grain and other food to supply his army; also that all the people who had buried or otherwise concealed gold and silver, or other treasures, should bring them forth again and give them up, or else make known where they were concealed. This the people promised that they would do.

After having entered the town, Genghis Khan was riding about the streets on horseback at the head of his troop of guards when he came to a large and very beautiful edifice. The doors were wide, and he drove his horse directly in. His troops, and the other soldiers who were there, followed him in. There were also with him some of the magistrates of the town, who were accompanying him in his progress about the city.

After the whole party had entered the edifice, Genghis Khan looked around, and then asked them, in a jeering manner, if that was the sultan's palace.

"No," said they, "it is the house of God."

The building was a mosque.

On hearing this, Genghis Khan alighted from his horse, and, giving the bridle to one of the principal magistrates to hold, he went up, in a very irreverent manner, to a sacred place where the priests were accustomed to sit. He seized the copy of the Koran which he found there, and threw it down under the feet of the horses. After amusing himself for a time in desecrating the temple by these and other similar performances, he caused his soldiers to bring in their provisions, and allowed them to eat and drink in the temple, in a riotous manner, without any regard to the sacredness of the place, or to the feelings of the people of the town which he outraged by this conduct.

A few days after this Genghis Khan assembled all the magistrates and principal citizens of the town, and made a speech to them from an elevated stand or pulpit which was erected for the purpose. He began his speech by praising God, and claiming to be an object of his special favor, in proof of which he recounted the victories which he had obtained, as he said, through the Divine aid. He then went on to denounce the perfidious conduct of the sultan toward him in making a solemn treaty of peace with him and then treacherously murdering his merchants and ambassadors. He said that the sultan was a detestable tyrant, and that God had commissioned him to rid the earth of all such monsters. He said, in conclusion, that he would protect their lives, and would not allow his soldiers to take away their household goods, provided they surrendered to him fairly and honestly all their money and other treasures; and if any of them refused to do this, or to tell where their treasures were hid, he would put them to the torture, and compel them to tell.

The wretched inhabitants of the town, feeling that they were entirely at the mercy of the terrible hordes that were in possession of the city, did not attempt to conceal anything. They brought forward their hidden treasures, and even offered their household goods to the conqueror if he was disposed to take them. They were only anxious to save, if possible, their dwellings and their lives. Genghis Khan appeared at first to be pleased with the submissive spirit which they manifested, but at last, under pretense that he heard of some soldiers being concealed somewhere, and perhaps irritated at the citadel's holding out so long against him, he ordered the town to be set on fire. The buildings were almost all of wood, and the fire raged among them with great fury. Multitudes of the inhabitants perished in the flames, and great numbers died miserably afterward from want and exposure. The citadel immediately afterward surrendered, and it would seem that Genghis Khan began to feel satisfied with the amount of misery which he had caused, for it is said that he spared the lives of the governor and of the soldiers, although we might have expected that he would have massacred them all.

The citadel was, however, demolished, and thus the town itself, and all that pertained to it, became a mass of smoking ruins. The property pillaged from the inhabitants was divided among the Mongul troops, while the people themselves went away, to roam as vagabonds and beggars over the surrounding country, and to die of want and despair.

119

What difference is there between such a conqueror as this and the captain of a band of pirates or of robbers, except in the immense magnitude of the scale on which he perpetrates his crimes?

The satisfaction which Genghis Khan felt at the capture of Bokhara was greatly increased by the intelligence which he received soon afterward from the two princes whom he had sent to lay siege to Otrar, informing him that that city had fallen into their hands, and that the governor of it, the officer who had so treacherously put to death the ambassadors and the merchants, had been taken and slain. The name of this governor was Gayer Khan. The sultan, knowing that Genghis Khan would doubtless make this city one of his first objects of attack, left the governor a force of fifty thousand men to defend it. He afterward sent him an additional force of ten thousand men, under the command of a general named Kariakas.

With these soldiers the governor shut himself up in the city. He knew very well that if he surrendered or was taken he could expect no mercy, and he went to work accordingly strengthening the fortifications, and laying in stores of provisions, determined to fight to the last extremity. The captain of the guard who came to assist him had not the same reason for being so very obstinate in the defense of the town, and this difference in the situation of the two commanders led to difficulty in the end, as we shall presently see.

The Mongul princes began the siege of Otrar by filling up the ditches that encircled the outer wall of the town in the places where they wished to plant their battering-rams to make breaches in the walls. They were hindered a great deal in their work, as is usual in such cases, by the sallies of the besieged, who rushed upon them in the night in great numbers, and with such desperate fury that they often succeeded in destroying some of the engines, or setting them on fire before they could be driven back into the town. This continued for some time, until at last the Mongul princes began to be discouraged, and they sent word to their father, who was then engaged in the siege of Bokhara, informing him of the desperate defense which was made by the garrison of Otrar, and asking his permission to turn the siege into a blockade—that is, to withdraw from the immediate vicinity of the walls, and to content themselves with investing the city closely on every side, so as to prevent any one from going out or coming in, until the provisions of the town should be exhausted, and the garrison be starved into a surrender. In this way, they said, the lives of vast numbers of the troops would be saved.

But their father sent back word to them that they must do no such thing, but must go on and _fight their way_ into the town, no matter how many of the men were killed.

So the princes began again with fresh ardor, and they pushed forward their operations with such desperate energy that in less than a month the outer wall, and the works of the besieged to defend it, were all in ruins. The towers were beaten down, the ramparts were broken, and many breaches were made through which the besiegers might be expected at any moment to force their way into the town. The besieged were accordingly obliged to abandon the outer walls and retire within the inner lines.

The Monguls now had possession of the suburbs, and, after pillaging them of all that they could convert to their own use, and burning and destroying everything else, they advanced to attack the inner works; and here the contest between the besiegers and the garrison was renewed more fiercely than ever. The besieged continued their resistance for five months, defending themselves by every possible means from the walls, and making desperate sallies from time to time in order to destroy the Monguls' engines and kill the men.

At length Kariakas, the captain of the guard, who had been sent to assist the governor in the defense of the town, began to think it was time that the carnage should cease and that the town should be surrendered. But the governor, who knew that he would most assuredly be beheaded if in any way he fell into the hands of the enemy, would not listen to any proposal of the kind. He succeeded, also, in exciting among the people of the town, and among the soldiers of the garrison, such a hatred of the Monguls, whom he represented as infidels of the very worst character, the enemies alike of God and man, that they joined him in the determination not to surrender.

Kariakas now found himself an object of suspicion and distrust in the town and in the garrison on account of his having made the proposal to surrender, and feeling that he was not safe, he determined to make a separate peace for himself and his ten thousand by going out secretly in the night and giving himself up to the princes. He thought that by doing this, and by putting the Monguls in possession of the gate through which his troops were to march out, so as to enable them to gain admission to the city, his life would be spared, and that he might perhaps be admitted into the service of Genghis Khan.

But he was mistaken in this idea. The princes said that a man who would betray his own countrymen would betray _them_ if he ever had a good opportunity. So they ordered him and all his officers to be slain, and the men to be divided among the soldiers as slaves.

They nevertheless took possession of the gate by which the deserters had come out, and by this means gained admission to the city. The governor fled to the citadel with all the men whom he could assemble, and shut himself up in it. Here he fought desperately for a month, making continual sallies at the head of

121

his men, and doing everything that the most resolute and reckless bravery could do to harass and beat off the besiegers. But all was in vain. In the end the walls of the citadel were so broken down by the engines brought to bear upon them, that one day the Monguls, by a determined and desperate assault made on all sides simultaneously, forced their way in, through the most dreadful scenes of carnage and destruction, and began killing without mercy every soldier that they could find.

The soldiers defended themselves to the last. Some took refuge in narrow courts and lanes, and on the roofs of the houses—for the citadel was so large that it formed of itself quite a little town—and fought desperately till they were brought down by the arrows of the Monguls. The governor took his position, in company with two men who were with him, on a terrace of his palace, and refused to surrender, but fought on furiously, determined to kill anyone who attempted to come near him. His wife was near, doing all in her power to encourage and sustain him.

Genghis Khan had given orders to the princes not to kill the governor, but to take him alive. He wished to have the satisfaction of disposing of him himself. For this reason the soldiers who attempted to take him on the terrace were very careful not to shoot their arrows at him, but only at the men who were with him, and while they did so a great many of them were killed by the arrows which the governor and his two friends discharged at those who attempted to climb up to the place where they were standing.

THE GOVERNOR ON THE TERRACE.

After a while the two men were killed, but the governor remained alive. Yet nobody could come near him. Those that attempted it were shot, and fell back again among their companions below. The governor's wife supplied him with arrows as fast as he could use them. At length all the arrows were spent, and then she brought him stones, which he hurled down upon his assailants when they tried to climb up to him. But at last so many ascended together that the governor could not beat them all back, and he was at length surrounded and secured, and immediately put in irons.

The princes wrote word at once to their father that the town was taken, and that the governor was in their hands a prisoner. They received orders in return to bring him with them to Bokhara. While on the way, however, another order came requiring them to put the prisoner to death, and this order was immediately executed.

What was the fate of his courageous and devoted wife has never been known.

CHAPTER 20: BATTLES AND SIEGES
1219-1220

Continuation of the war—Saganak—Hassan—The murdered ambassador—Jughi's revenge—Jughi's general policy—Account of a stratagem—The town taken—A beautiful city—Toukat—Toukat taken—Arrangements for plundering it—Kojend—Timur Melek—His preparations for defense—Engines and battering-rams—The floating batteries—The morass—Obstinate conflict—The pretended deserters—No more stones—Building of the jetty—The horsemen in the water—Timur's boats—The fire-proof awnings—The fire-boats and the bridge—The bridge burned—Pursuit—Battle in the river—The boats aground—Timur's adventures—He finally escapes—The governor's family—Kojend surrendered.

After the fall of Bokhara and Otrar, the war was continued for two years with great vigor by Genghis Khan and the Monguls, and the poor sultan was driven from place to place by his merciless enemies, until at last his cause was wholly lost, and he himself, as will appear in the next chapter, came to a miserable end.

During the two years while Genghis Khan continued the war against him, a great many incidents occurred illustrating the modes of warfare practiced in those days, and the sufferings which were endured by the mass of the people in consequence of these terrible struggles between rival despots contending for the privilege of governing them.

At one time Genghis Khan sent his son Jughi with a large detachment to besiege and take a certain town named Saganak. As soon as Jughi arrived before the place, he sent in a flag of truce to call upon the people of the town to surrender, promising, at the same time, to treat them kindly if they would do so.

The bearer of the flag was a Mohammedan named Hassan. Jughi probably thought that the message would be better received by the people of the town if brought to them by one of their own countrymen, but he made a great mistake in this. The people, instead of being pleased with the messenger because he was a Mohammedan, were very much exasperated against him. They considered him a renegade and a traitor; and, although the governor had solemnly promised that he should be allowed to go and come in safety, so great a tumult arose that the governor found it impossible to protect him, and the poor man was torn to pieces by the mob.

Jughi immediately assaulted the town with all his force, and as soon as he got possession of it he slaughtered without mercy all the officers and soldiers of the garrison, and killed also about one half of the inhabitants, in order to avenge the death of his murdered messenger. He also caused a handsome monument to be erected to his memory in the principal square of the town.

Jughi treated the inhabitants of every town that dared to resist with extreme severity, while those that yielded at once were, in some degree, spared and protected. The consequence of this policy was that the people of many of the towns surrendered without attempting to defend themselves at all. In one case the magistrates and other principal inhabitants of a town came out to meet him a distance of two days' journey from them, bringing with them the keys of the town, and a great quantity of magnificent presents, all of which they laid at the conqueror's feet, and implored his mercy.

There was one town which Jughi's force took by a kind of stratagem. A certain engineer, whom he employed to make a reconnoissance of the fortifications, reported that there was a place on one side of the town where there was a ditch full of water outside of the wall, which made the access to the wall there so difficult that the garrison would not be at all likely to expect an attack on that side. The engineer proposed a plan for building some light bridges, which the soldiers were to throw over the ditch in the night, after having drawn off the attention of the garrison to some other quarter, and then, mounting upon the walls by means of ladders, to get into the town. This plan was adopted. The bridges and the ladders were prepared, and then, when the appointed night came, a feigned attack was made in the opposite part of the town. The garrison were then all called off to repel this pretended attack, and in this way the wall opposite to the ditch was left undefended. The soldiers then threw the bridges over the ditch, and planted the ladders against the wall, and before the garrison could get intelligence of what they were doing they had made their way into the town, and had opened one of the gates, and by this means the whole army got in. The engineer himself, who had proposed the plan, went up first on the first ladder that was planted against the wall. To take the lead in such an escalade required great coolness and courage, for it was dark, and no one knew, in going up the ladder, how many enemies he might have to encounter at the top of it.

The next place which the army of Jughi approached was a quiet and beautiful town, the seat of several institutions of learning, and the residence of learned men and men of leisure. It was a very pleasant place, full of fountains, gardens, and delightful pleasure-grounds, with many charming public and private promenades. The name of this place was Toukat, and the beauty and attractiveness of it were proverbial through all the country.

Toukat was a place rather of pleasure than of strength, and yet it was surrounded by a wall, and the governor of it determined to make an effort to defend it. The garrison fought bravely, and they kept the besiegers off for three days. At the end of that time the engines of the Monguls had made so many breaches in the walls that the governor was convinced that they would soon get in, and so he sent to Jughi to ask for the terms on which he would allow them to surrender. Jughi replied that he would not now make any terms with him at all. It was too late. He ought to have surrendered at the beginning.

So the Mongul army forced its way into the town, and slaughtered the whole garrison without mercy. Jughi then ordered all the inhabitants, men, women, and children, to repair to a certain place on the plain outside the walls. In obedience to this command, all the people went to the appointed place. They went with fear and trembling, expecting that they were all to be killed. But they found, in the end, that the object of Jughi in bringing them thus out of the town was not to kill them, but only to call them away from the houses, so that the soldiers could plunder them more conveniently while the owners were away. After being kept out of the town for a time they were allowed to return, and when they went back to their houses they found that they had been pillaged and stripped of everything that the soldiers could carry away.

There was another large and important town named Kojend. It was situated two or three hundred miles to the northward of Samarcand, on the River Sir, which flows into Aral Lake. The governor of this city was Timur Melek. He was a very powerful chieftain, and a man of great military renown, having often been in active service under the sultan as one of the principal generals of his army. When Timur heard of the fall of Toukat, he presumed that his city of Kojend would be next attacked, as it seemed to come next in the way of the Mongul army; so he began to make vigorous preparations for defense. He broke up all the roads leading toward the town, and destroyed the bridges. He also laid in great supplies of food to maintain the inhabitants in case of a protracted siege, and he ordered all the corn, fruits, and cattle of the surrounding country, which he did not require for this purpose, to be taken away and stowed in secret places at a distance, to prevent their falling into the hands of the enemy.

Jughi did not himself attack this town, but sent a large detachment under the orders of a general named Elak Nevian. Elak advanced toward the city and commenced his operations. The first thing that was to be done was to rebuild a bridge over the river, so as to enable him to gain access to the town, which was on the opposite bank. Then he set up immense engines at different points along the line, some of which were employed to batter down the walls, and others, at the same time, to throw stones, darts, and arrows over the parapets, in order to drive the garrison back from them. These engines did great execution. Those built to batter down the walls were of great size and power. Some of them, it was said, threw stones over the wall as big as millstones.

Timur Melek was equally active in the defense of the town. He built a number of flat-bottomed boats, which might be called floating batteries, since they were constructed for throwing missiles of all sorts into the camp of the enemy. These batteries, it is said, were covered over on the top to protect the men, and they had port-holes in the sides, like a modern man-of-war, out of which, not cannon balls and bomb-shells indeed, but arrows, darts, javelins, and stones were projected. The boats were sent out, some on the upper side of the town and some on the lower, and were placed in stations where they could most effectually reach the Mongul works. They were the means of killing and wounding great multitudes of men, and they greatly disturbed and hindered the besiegers' operations.

Still Elak persevered. He endeavored to shut up the city on every side as closely as possible; but there was on one side a large morass or jungle which he could not guard, and Timur received a great many re-enforcements, to take the place of the men who were killed on the walls, by that way. In the mean time, however, Elak was continually receiving re-enforcements too from Prince Jughi, who was not at a great distance, and thus the struggle was continued with great fury.

At last Timur contrived an ingenious stratagem, by which he hoped to cause his enemy to fall into a snare. It seems that there was a small island in the river, not far from the walls of the city, on which, before the siege commenced, Timur had built a fortress, to be held as a sort of advanced post, and had garrisoned the fortress with about one thousand men. Timur now, in order to divert the attention of the Monguls from the city itself, sent a number of men out from the city, who pretended to be deserters, and went immediately to the Mongul camp. Of course, Elak questioned them about the defenses of the city, in order to learn where the weak points were for him to attack. The pretended deserters advised him to attack this fortress on the island, saying that it could very easily be taken, and that its situation was such that, when it was taken, the city itself must surrender, for it completely commanded the place.

So Elak caused his principal engines to be removed to the bank of the river, opposite the island, and employed all his energies and spent all his ammunition in shooting at the fortress; but the river was so wide, and the walls of the fortress wore so thick and so high, that he made very little impression. At last his whole supply of stones—for stones served in those days instead of cannon balls—was exhausted, and as the town was situated in an alluvial district, in which no stones were to be found, he was obliged to send ten or twelve miles to the upland to procure a fresh supply of ammunition. All this consumed much time, and enabled the garrison to recruit themselves a great deal and to strengthen their defenses.

The operations of the siege were in a great measure suspended while the men were obtaining a new supply of stones, and the whole disposable force of the army was employed in going back and forth to bring them. At length an immense quantity were collected; but then the Mongul general changed his plan. Instead of throwing the stones from his engines toward the fortress on the island, which it had been proved was beyond his reach, he determined to build out a jetty into the river toward it, so as to get a stand-point for his engines nearer the walls, where they could have some chance of doing execution. So he set his men at work to prepare fascines, and bundles, and rafts of timber, which were to be loaded with the stones and sunk in the river to form the foundation for the proposed bank. The men would bring the stones down to the bank in their hands, and then horsemen, who were ready on the brink, would take them, and, resting them on the saddle, would drive their horses in until they came near the place where the stones were to go, when they would throw them down and then return for others. In this way they could work upon the jetty in many parts at once, some being employed in building at the end where it abutted on the shore, while the horsemen were laying the foundations at the same time out in the middle of the stream. The work of the horsemen was very difficult and dangerous, on account of holes in the sandy bottom of the river, into which they were continually sinking. Besides this, the garrison on the walls were doing their utmost all the time to impede the work by shooting arrows, javelins, stones, and fiery darts among the workmen, by which means vast numbers, both of men and horses, were killed.

The Monguls, however, persevered, and, notwithstanding all the opposition which the garrison made, they succeeded in advancing the mole which they were building so far that Timur was convinced that they would soon gain so advantageous a position that it would be impossible for him to hold out against them. So he determined to attempt to make his escape. His plan was to embark on board his boats, with all his men, and go down the river in the night.

In order to prepare for this undertaking, he employed his men secretly in building more boats, until he had in all more than seventy. These boats were kept out of sight, in hidden places in the river, until all were ready. Each of them was covered with a sort of heavy awning or roof, made of wet felt, which was plastered over with a coating of clay and vinegar. This covering was intended both to defend the men from missiles and the boats themselves from being set on fire.

There was one obstacle to the escape of the boats which it was necessary to remove beforehand, and that was the bridge which the Monguls had built across the river, just below the town, when they first came to besiege it. To destroy this bridge, Timur one night made a sally from one of the gates, and attacked the men who were stationed to guard the bridge. At the same time he sent down the current of the river a number of great flat-bottomed boats, filled with combustibles of various kinds, mixed with tar and naphtha. These combustibles were set on fire before they were launched, and, as the current of the river bore them down one after another against the bridge, they set the wooden piers and posts that supported it on fire, while the guard, being engaged with the party which had sallied from the town, could not go to extinguish the flames, and thus the bridge was consumed.

The way being thus opened, Timur Melek very soon afterward embarked his family and the greater part of his army on board the boats in the night; and, while the Monguls had no suspicion of what was going on, the boats were launched, and sent off one after another swiftly down the stream. Before morning came all traces of the party had passed away.

Very soon, however, the Mongul general heard how his intended prey had escaped him, and he immediately sent off a strong detachment to follow the southern bank of the river and pursue the fugitives. The detachment soon overtook them, and then a furious battle ensued between the Mongul horsemen on the banks and in the margin of the water and the men in the boats, who kept the boats all the time as near as possible to the northern shore.

Sometimes, however, when the stream was narrow, or when a rocky point projected from the northern shore, so as to drive the boats nearer to the Mongul side, the battle became very fierce and bloody. The Monguls drove their horses far into the water, so as to be as near as possible to the boats, and threw arrows, javelins, and fiery darts at them, while the Mohammedans defended themselves as well as they could from their windows or port-holes.

BATTLE OF THE BOATS.

[Illustration: BATTLE OF THE BOATS.]

Things went on in this way for some time, until, at length, the boats arrived at a part of the river where the water was so shallow—being obstructed by sand-bars and shoals—that the boats fell aground. There was nothing now for Timur to do but to abandon the boats and escape with his men to the land. This he succeeded in doing; and, after reaching the shore, he was able to form his men in array, on an elevated piece of ground, before Elak could bring up a sufficient number of men to attack him.

When the Monguls at length came to attack him, he beat them off in the first instance, but he was obliged soon afterward to leave the field and continue his retreat. Of course, he was hotly pursued by the Monguls. His men became rapidly thinned in number, some being killed, and others getting separated from the main body in the confusion of the flight, until, at last, Timur was left almost alone. At last he was himself on the very point of being taken. There were three Monguls closely pursuing him. He turned round and shot an arrow at the foremost of the pursuers. The arrow struck the Mongul in the eye. The agony which the wounded man felt was so great that the two others stopped to assist him, and in the mean time Timur got out of the way. In due time, and after meeting with some other hairbreadth escapes, he reached the camp of the sultan, who received him very joyfully, loaded him with praises for the indomitable spirit which he had evinced, and immediately made him governor of another city.

In the mean time, some of the boats which had been abandoned by the soldiers were got off by the men who had been left in charge of them—one especially, which contained the family of Timur. This boat went quietly down the river, and conveyed the family to a place of safety.

The city of Kojend, from which Timur and his men had fled, was, of course, now without any means of defense, and it surrendered the very next day to the Monguls.

CHAPTER 21: DEATH OF THE SULTAN
1220

Pursuit of the sultan—The two ladies—Character of the queen-mother—Khatun—Her retirement—Samarcand—Fortifications of the place—Water-works—Gates and towers—Crowds of people seeking refuge—Encampment—Arrival of the Monguls—Dissensions within the city—A deputation—Massacre—Escape of the governor—Forlorn condition of the sultan—The sultan sends away his treasures—His flight and his despondency—Narrow escape—Rage of his pursuers—Visit from his son Jalaloddin—His dying words—Death and burial—Khatun at Karazm—Her cruelty to her captives—Dissension—Khatun's escape—Her obstinacy—Cause of her hatred of Jalaloddin—The siege of the fortress—The governor's hopes—Want of rain—Great suffering—The queen made captive—Cruel treatment of the queen-mother.

In the mean time, while Jughi and the other generals were ravaging the country with their detachments, and besieging and capturing all the secondary towns and fortresses that came in their way, as related in the last chapter, Genghis Khan himself, with the main body of the army, had advanced to Samarcand in pursuit of the sultan, who had, as he supposed, taken shelter there. Samarcand was the capital of the country, and was then, as it has been since, a great and renowned city.

Besides the sultan himself, whom Genghis Khan was pursuing, there were the ladies of his family whom he wished also to capture. The two principal ladies were the sultana and the queen-mother. The queen-mother was a lady of very great distinction. She had been greatly renowned during the lifetime of her husband, the former sultan, for her learning, her piety, the kindness of her heart, and the general excellence of her character, so far as her dealings with her subjects and friends were concerned, and her influence throughout the realm had been unbounded. At some periods of her life she had exercised a great deal of political power, and at one time she bore the very grand title of _Protectress of the faith of the world_. She exercised the power which she then possessed, in the main, in a very wise and beneficial manner. She administered justice impartially. She protected the weak, and restrained the oppressions of the strong. She listened to all the cases which were brought before her with great attention and patience, and arrived almost always at just conclusions respecting them. With all this, however, she was very strict and severe, and, as has almost always been the case with women raised to the possession of irresponsible power, she was unrelenting and cruel in the extreme whenever, as she judged, any political necessity required her to act with decision. Her name was Khatun.[E]

[Footnote E: Pronounced _Cah-toon_.]

Khatun was not now at Samarcand. She was at Karazm, a city which was the chief residence of the court. She had been living there in retirement ever since the death of her husband, the present sultan's father.

Samarcand itself, as has already been said, was a great and splendid city. Like most of the other cities, it was inclosed in a double wall, though, in this case, the outer wall surrounded the whole city, while the inner one inclosed the mosque, the palace of the sultan, and some other public buildings. These walls were much better built and more strongly fortified than those of Bokhara. There were twelve iron gates, it is said, in the outer wall. These gates were a league apart from each other. At every two leagues along the wall was a fort capable of containing a large body of men. The walls were likewise strengthened with battlements and towers, in which the men could fight under shelter, and they were surrounded by a broad and deep ditch, to prevent an enemy from approaching too near to them, in order to undermine them or batter them down.

The city was abundantly supplied with water by means of hydraulic constructions as perfect and complete as could be made in those days. The water was brought by leaden pipes from a stream which came down from the mountains at some distance from the town. It was conveyed by these pipes to every part of the town, and was distributed freely, so that every great street had a little current of water running through it, and every house a fountain in the court or garden. Besides this, in a public square or park there was a mound where the water was made to spout up in the centre, and then flow down in little rivulets and cascades on every side.

The gates and towers which have been described were in the outer wall, and beyond them, in the environs, were a great many fields, gardens, orchards, and beautifully-cultivated grounds, which produced fruits of all sorts, that were sent by the merchants into all the neighboring countries. At a little distance the town was almost entirely concealed from view by these gardens and orchards, there being nothing to be seen but minarets, and some of the loftier roofs of the houses, rising above the tops of the trees.

There were so many people who flocked into Samarcand from the surrounding country for shelter and protection, when they learned that Genghis Khan was coming, that the place would hardly contain them. In addition to these, the sultan sent over one hundred thousand troops to defend the town, with thirty generals to command them. There were twenty large elephants, too, that were brought with the army, to be employed in any service which might be required of them during the siege. This army, however, instead of entering the city at once, encamped about it. They strengthened the position of the camp by a deep ditch which they dug, throwing up the earth from the ditch on the side toward the camp so as to form a redoubt with which to defend the ground from the Monguls. But as soon as Genghis Khan arrived they were speedily driven from this post, and forced to take shelter within the walls of the city. Here they defended themselves with so much vigor and resolution that Genghis Khan would probably have found it very difficult to take the town had it not been for dissensions within the walls. It seems that the rich merchants and other wealthy men of the city, being convinced that the place would sooner or later fall into the hands of the Monguls, thought it would be better to surrender it at once, while they were in a condition to make some terms by which they might hope to save their lives, and perhaps their property.

But the generals would not listen to any proposition of this kind. They had been sent by the sultan to defend the town, and they felt bound in honor, in obedience to their orders, to fight in defense of it to the last extremity.

The dissension within the city grew more and more violent every day, until at length the party of the inhabitants grew so strong and decided that they finally took possession of one of the gates, and sent a large deputation, consisting of priests, magistrates, and some of the principal citizens, to Genghis Khan, bearing with them the keys of the town, and proposing to deliver them up to him if he would spare the garrison and the inhabitants. But he said he would make no terms except with those who were of their party and were willing to surrender. In respect to the generals and the soldiers of the garrison he would make no promises.

The deputation gave up the keys and Genghis Khan entered the city. The inhabitants were spared, but the soldiers were massacred wherever they could be found. A great many perished in the streets. A considerable body of them, however, with the governor at their head, retreated within the inner wall, and there defended themselves desperately for four days. At the end of that time, finding that their case was hopeless, and knowing that they could expect no quarter from the Monguls in any event, they resolved to make a sally and cut their way through the ranks of their enemies at all hazards. The governor, accordingly, put himself at the head of a troop of one thousand horse, and, coming out suddenly from his retreat, he dashed through the camp at a time when the Monguls were off their guard, and so gained the open country and made his escape. All the soldiers that remained behind in the city were immediately put to the sword.

In the mean time, the sultan himself, finding that his affairs were going to ruin, retreated from province to province, accompanied by as large a force as he could keep together, and vainly seeking to find some place of safety. He had several sons, and among them two whose titles were Jalaloddin and Kothboddin. Jalaloddin was the oldest, and was therefore naturally entitled to be his father's successor; but, for some reason or other, the queen-mother, Khatun, had taken a dislike to him, and had persuaded her son, the sultan, to execute a sort of act or deed by which Jalaloddin was displaced, and Kothboddin, who was a great favorite of hers, was made heir to the throne in his place.

The sultan had other sons who were governors of different provinces, and he fled from one to another of these, seeking in vain for some safe retreat. But he could find none. He was hunted from place to place by detachments of the Monguls, and the number of his attendants and followers was continually diminishing, until at last he began to be completely discouraged.

At length, at one of the cities where he made a short stay, he delivered to an officer named Omar, who was the steward of his household, ten coffers sealed with the royal signet, with instructions to take them secretly to a certain distant fortress and lock them up carefully there, without allowing any one to know that he did it.

These coffers contained the royal jewels, and they were of inestimable value.

After this, one of his sons joined him with quite a large force, but very soon a large body of Monguls came up, and, after a furious battle, the sultan's troops were defeated and scattered in all directions; and he was again obliged to fly, accompanied by a very small body of officers, who still contrived to keep near him. With these he succeeded, at last, in reaching a very retired town near the Caspian Sea, where he hoped to remain concealed. His strength was now spent, and all his courage gone. He sank down into a condition of the greatest despondency and distress, and spent his time in going to the mosque and offering up prayers to God to save him from total ruin. He made confession of his sins, and promised an entire amendment of life if the Almighty would deliver him from his enemies and restore him to his throne.

At last the Mongul detachment that was in pursuit of him in that part of the country were informed by a peasant where he was; and one day, while he was at his prayers in the mosque, word was brought to him that the Monguls were coming. He rushed out of the mosque, and, guided by some friends, ran down to the shore and got into a boat, with a view of escaping by sea, all retreat by land being now cut off.

He had scarce got on board the boat when the Monguls appeared on the shore. The men in the boat immediately pushed off. The Monguls, full of disappointment and rage, shot at them with their arrows; but the sultan was not struck by any of them, and was soon out of the reach of his pursuers.

The sultan lay in the boat almost helpless, being perfectly exhausted by the terror and distress which he had endured. He soon began to suffer, too, from an intense pain in the chest and side, which gradually became so severe that he could scarcely breathe. The men with him in the boat, finding that he was seriously sick, made the best of their way to a small island named Abiskun, which is situated near the southeastern corner of the sea. Here they pitched a tent, and made up a bed in it, as well as they could, for the sufferer. They also sent a messenger to the shore to bring off a physician secretly. The physician did all that was in his power, but it was too late. The inflammation and the pain subsided after a time, but it was evident that the patient was sinking, and that he was about to die.

It happened that the sultan's son, Jalaloddin, the one who had been set aside in favor of his brother Kothboddin, was at this time on the main land not far from the island, and intelligence was communicated to him of his father's situation. He immediately went to the island to see him, taking with him two of his brothers. They were obliged to manage the business very secretly, to prevent the Monguls from finding out what was going on.

On the arrival of Jalaloddin, the sultan expressed great satisfaction in seeing him, and he revoked the decree by which he had been superseded in the succession.

"You, my son," said he, "are, after all, the one among all my children who is best able to revenge me on the Monguls; therefore I revoke the act which I formerly executed at the request of the queen, my mother, in favor of Kothboddin."

He then solemnly appointed Jalaloddin to be his successor, and enjoined upon the other princes to be obedient and faithful to him as their sovereign. He also formally delivered to him his sword as the emblem and badge of the supreme power which he thus conferred upon him.

Soon after this the sultan expired. The attendants buried the body secretly on the island for fear of the Monguls. They washed it carefully before the interment, according to custom, and then put on again a portion of the same dress which the sultan had worn when living, having no means of procuring or making any other shroud.

As for Khatun, the queen-mother, when she heard the tidings of her son's death, and was informed, at the same time, that her favorite Kothboddin had been set aside, and Jalaloddin, whom she hated, and who, she presumed, hated her, had been made his successor, she was in a great rage. She was at that time at

Karazm, which was the capital, and she attempted to persuade the officers and soldiers near her not to submit to the sultan's decree, but to make Kothboddin their sovereign after all.

While she was engaged in forming this conspiracy, the news reached the city that the Monguls were coming. Khatun immediately determined to flee to save her life. She had, it seems, in her custody at Karazm twelve children, the sons of various princes that reigned in different parts of the empire or in the environs of it. These children were either held as hostages, or had been made captive in insurrections and wars, and were retained in prison as a punishment to their fathers. The queen-mother found that she could not take these children with her, and so she ordered them all to be slain. She was afraid that the Monguls, when they came, might set them free.

As soon as she was gone the city fell into great confusion on account of the struggles for power between the two parties of Jalaloddin and Kothboddin. But the sultana, who had made the mischief, did not trouble herself to know how it would end. Her only anxiety was to save her own life. After various wanderings and adventures, she at last found her way into a very retired district of country lying on the southern shore of the Caspian, between the mountains and the sea, and here she sought refuge in a castle or fortress named Ilan, where she thought she was secure from all pursuit. She brought with her to the castle her jewels and all her most valuable treasures.

But Genghis Khan had spies in every part of the country, and he was soon informed where Khatun was concealed. So he sent a messenger to a certain Mongul general named Hubbe Nevian, who was commanding a detachment in that part of the country, informing him that Khatun was in the castle of Ilan, and commanding him to go and lay siege to it, and to take it at all hazards, and to bring Khatun to him either dead or alive.

Hubbe immediately set off for the castle. The queen mother, however, had notice of his approach, and the lords who were with her urged her to fly. If she would go with them, they said, they would take her to Jalaloddin, and he would protect her. But she would not listen to any such proposal. She hated Jalaloddin so intensely that she would not, even to save her life, put herself under his power. The very worst possible treatment, she said, that she could receive from the Monguls would be more agreeable to her than the greatest favors from the hand of Jalaloddin.

The ground of this extreme animosity which she felt toward Jalaloddin was not any personal animosity to _him_; it arose simply from an ancient and long-continued dislike and hatred which she had borne against his mother!

So Khatun refused to retire from the danger, and soon afterward the horde of Monguls arrived, and pitched their camp before the castle walls.

For three months Hubbe and his Monguls continued to ply the walls of the fortress with battering-rams and other engines, in order to force their way in, but in vain. The place was too strong for them. At length Genghis Khan, hearing how the case stood, sent word to them to give up the attempt to make a breach, and to invest the place closely on all sides, so as to allow no person to go out or to come in; in that way, he said, the garrison would soon be starved into a surrender.

When the governor of the castle saw, by the arrangements which Hubbe made in obedience to this order, that this was the course that was to be pursued, he said he was not uneasy, for his magazines were full of provisions, and as to water, the rain which fell very copiously there among the mountains always afforded an abundant supply.

But the governor was mistaken in his calculations in respect to the rain. It usually fell very frequently in that region, but after the blockade of the fortress commenced, for three weeks there was not the smallest shower. The people of the country around thought this failure of the rain was a special judgment of heaven against the queen for the murder of the children, and for her various other crimes. It was, indeed, remarkable, for in ordinary times the rain was so frequent that the people of all that region depended upon it entirely for their supply of water, and never found it necessary to search for springs or to dig wells.

The sufferings of the people within the fortress for want of water were very great. Many of them died in great misery, and at length the provisions began to fail too, and Khatun was compelled to allow the governor to surrender.

The Monguls immediately seized the queen, and took possession of all her treasures. They also took captive all the lords and ladies who had attended her, and the women of her household, and two or three of her great-grandchildren, whom she had brought with her in her flight. All these persons were sent under a strong guard to Genghis Khan.

Genghis Khan retained the queen as a captive for some time, and treated her in a very cruel and barbarous manner. He would sometimes order her to be brought into his tent, at the end of his dinner, that he might enjoy his triumph by insulting and deriding her. On these occasions he would throw her scraps of food from the table as if she had been a dog.

He took away the children from her too, all but one, whom he left with her a while to comfort her, as he said; but one day an officer came and seized this one from her very arms, while she was dressing him and combing his hair. This last blow caused her a severer pang than any that she had before endured, and left her utterly disconsolate and heart-broken.

Some accounts say that soon after this she was put to death, but others state that Genghis Khan retained her several years as a captive, and carried her to and fro in triumph in his train through the countries over which she had formerly reigned with so much power and splendor. She deserved her sufferings, it is true; but Genghis Khan was none the less guilty, on that account, for treating her so cruelly.

CHAPTER 22: VICTORIOUS CAMPAIGNS
1220-1221

Continued conquests—Efforts of Jalaloddin—Jalaloddin becomes discouraged—The governor's advice—Renewed exertions—Stratagem—Fictitious soldiers—Quarrel about a horse—Disaffection—Jalaloddin's forces divided—Great battle in the defile—Orders to take Jalaloddin alive—He takes leave of his family—His escape across the river—His defiance of his pursuers—Struggles of the horse—Night spent in a tree—Jalaloddin meets with friends—Large body of men escaped—Pressing wants—Timely aid from Jamalarrazad—Fate of the sultan's family—Sunken treasures—Jalaloddin's end—Sieges—Logs instead of stones for ammunition—Modern bombs—Bringing stones—Occupation of slaves—Shields—Protection against fire—Precautions—Attempts at resistance—Account of Kubru—His noble spirit—Kubru slain—Pusillanimity—Sorties by the garrisons—Desperation of the people—Mode of disposing of prisoners—Prodigious slaughter—Atrocities—The pearl—Genghis Khan's grandson killed—His mother's revenge—Principles of the Mohammedan faith—Genghis Khan's opinion—The spirit of religious bigotry.

After this Genghis Khan went on successfully for several years, extending his conquests over all the western part of Central Asia, while the generals whom he had left at home were extending his dominions in the same manner in the eastern portion. He overran nearly all of Persia, went entirely around the Caspian Sea, and even approached the confines of India.

In this expedition toward India he was in pursuit of Jalaloddin. Immediately after the death of his father, Jalaloddin had done all in his power to raise an army and carry on the war against Genghis Khan. He met with a great deal of embarrassment and difficulty at first, on account of the plots and conspiracies which his grandmother had organized in favor of his brother Kothboddin, and the dissensions among his people to which they gave rise. At last, in the course of a year, he succeeded, in some measure, in healing this breach and in raising an army; and, though he was not strong enough to fight the Monguls in a general battle, he hung about them in their march and harassed them in various ways, so as to impede their operations very essentially. Genghis Khan from time to time sent off detachments from his army to take him. He was often defeated in the engagements which ensued, but he always succeeded in saving himself and in keeping together a portion of his men, and thus he maintained himself in the field, though he was growing weaker and weaker all the time.

At last he became completely discouraged, and, after signal defeat which he met with from a detachment which had been sent against him by Genghis Khan, he went, with the few troops that remained together, to a strong fortress among the mountains, and told the governor that it seemed to him useless to continue the struggle any longer, and that he had come to shut himself up in the fortress, and abandon the contest in despair.

The governor, however, told him that it was not right for a prince, the descendant of ancestors so illustrious as his, and the inheritor of so resplendent a crown, to yield to discouragement and despondency on account of the reverses of fortune. He advised him again to take the field, and to raise a new army, and continue the contest to the end.

Jalaloddin determined to follow this advice, and, after a brief period of repose at the castle, he again took the field.

He made great exertions, and finally succeeded in getting together about twenty thousand men. This was a small force, it is true, compared with the numbers of the enemy; but it was sufficient, if well managed, to enable the prince to undertake operations of considerable importance, and Jalaloddin began to feel somewhat encouraged again. With his twenty thousand men he gained one or two victories too, which encouraged him still more. In one of these cases he defeated rather a singular stratagem which the Mongul general contrived. It seems that the Mongul detachment which was sent out in this instance against Jalaloddin was not strong enough, and the general, in order to make Jalaloddin believe that his force was greater than it really was, ordered all the felt caps and cloaks that there were in the army to be stuffed with straw, and placed on the horses and camels of the baggage, in order to give the appearance of a second line of reserve in the rear of the line of real soldiers. This was to induce Jalaloddin to surrender without fighting.

But in some way or other Jalaloddin detected the deceit, and, instead of surrendering, fought the Monguls with great vigor, and defeated them. He gained a very decided victory, and perhaps this might have been the beginning of a change of fortune for him if, unfortunately, his generals had not quarreled about the division of the spoil. There was a beautiful Arabian horse which two of his leading generals desired to possess, and each claimed it. The dispute became, at last, so violent that one of the generals struck the other in his face with the lash of his whip. Upon this the feud became a deadly one. Both parties appealed to Jalaloddin. He did not wish to make either general an enemy by deciding in favor of the other, and so he tried to compromise the matter. He did not succeed in doing this; and one of the generals, mortally offended, went off in the night, taking with him all that portion of the troops which was under his command.

Jalaloddin did everything in his power to bring the disaffected general back again; but, before he could accomplish this purpose, Genghis Khan came up with a large force between the two parties, and prevented their effecting a junction.

Jalaloddin had now no alternative but to retreat. Genghis Khan followed him, and it was in this way that, after a time, both the armies reached the banks of the Indus, on the borders of India.

Jalaloddin, being closely pursued, took his position in a narrow defile near the bank of the river, and here a great battle was fought among the rocks and precipices. Jalaloddin, it is said, had only thirty thousand men at his command, while Genghis Khan was at the head of an army of three hundred thousand. The numbers in both cases are probably greatly exaggerated, but the proportion may perhaps be true.

It was only a small portion of the Mongul army that could get into the defile where the sultan's troops had posted themselves; and so desperately did the latter fight, that it is said they killed twenty thousand of the Monguls before they gave in. In fact, they fought like wild beasts, with desperate and unremitting fury, all day long. Toward night it became evident to Jalaloddin that it was all over with him. A large portion of his followers were killed. Some had made their escape across the river, though many of those who sought to do so were drowned in the attempt. The rest of his men were completely exhausted and discouraged, and wholly unable to renew the contest on the following day.

Jalaloddin had exposed himself very freely in the fight, in hopes, perhaps, that he should be killed. But Genghis Khan had given positive orders that he should be taken alive. He had even appointed two of his generals to watch carefully, and to see that no person should, under any circumstances, kill him. He wished to take him alive, in order to lead him through the country a prisoner, and exhibit him to his former subjects as a trophy of his victory, just as he had done and was still doing with the old queen Khatun, his grandmother.

But Jalaloddin was determined that his conqueror should not enjoy this pleasure. He resolved to attempt to save himself by swimming the river. He accordingly went first, breathless, and covered with dust and blood from the fight, to take a hurried leave of his mother, his wives, and his children, who, as was customary in those countries and times, had accompanied him in his campaign. He found them in his tent, full of anxiety and terror. He took leave of them with much sorrow and many tears, trying to comfort them with the hope that they should meet again in happier times. Then he took off his armor and his arms, in order that he might not be impeded in crossing the river, reserving, however, his sword and bow, and a quiver full of arrows. He then mounted a fresh horse and rode toward the river.

When he reached the bank of the river, the horse found the current so rapid and the agitation of the water so great that he was very unwilling to advance; but Jalaloddin spurred him in. Indeed, there was no time to be lost; for scarcely had he reached the shore when Genghis Khan himself, and a party of Monguls, appeared in view, advancing to seize him. They stopped on the bank when they saw Jalaloddin ride into the water among the rocks and whirlpools. They did not dare to follow him, but they remained at the water-side to see how his perilous adventure would end.

As soon as Jalaloddin found that he was out of their reach, he stopped at a place where his horse found a foothold, and turned round toward his pursuers with looks of hatred and defiance. He then drew his bow, and began to shoot at them with his arrows, and he continued to shoot until all the arrows in his quiver were exhausted. Some of the more daring of the Monguls proposed to Genghis Khan that they should swim out and try to take him. But Genghis Khan would not allow them to go. He said the attempt would be useless.

"You can do nothing at all with him," said he. "A man of such cool and determined bravery as that will defy and defeat all your attempts. Any father might be proud to have such a son, and any son proud to be descended from such a father."

When his arrows were all expended, Jalaloddin took to the river again; and his horse, after a series of most desperate struggles among the whirlpools and eddies, and the boiling surges which swept around the rocks, succeeded at length in carrying his master over. The progress of the horse was watched with great interest by Genghis Khan and his party from the shore as long as they could see him.

As soon as Jalaloddin landed, and had recovered a little from the fatigue and excitement of the passage, he began to look around him, and to consider what was next to be done. He found himself entirely alone, in a wild and solitary place, which he had reason to fear was infested with tigers and other ferocious beasts of prey, such as haunt the jungles in India. Night was coming on too, and there were no signs of any habitations or of any shelter. So he fastened his horse at the foot of a tree, and climbed up himself among the branches, and in this way passed the night.

The next morning he came down and began to walk along the bank of the river to see what he could find. He was in a state of great anxiety and distress. Suddenly, to his great relief and joy, he came upon a small troop of soldiers, accompanied by some officers, who had escaped across the river from the battle as he had done. Three of these officers were his particular friends, and he was overjoyed to see them. They had made their way across the river in a boat which they had found upon the bank at the beginning of the defeat of the army. They had spent the whole night in the boat, being in great danger from the shoals and shelving rocks, and from the impetuosity of the current. Finally, toward morning, they had landed, not far from the place where Jalaloddin found them.

Not long after this he came upon a troop of three hundred horsemen, who had escaped by swimming the river at a place where the water was more smooth, at some distance below. These men told him that about six miles farther down the stream there was a body of about four thousand men who had made their escape in a similar manner. On assembling these men, Jalaloddin found himself once more at the head of a considerable force.

The immediate wants of the men were, however, extremely pressing, for they were all wholly destitute of food and of every other necessary, and Jalaloddin would have been greatly embarrassed to provide for them had it not been for the thoughtfulness and fidelity of one of the officers of his household on the other side of the river. This officer's name was Jamalarrazad. As soon as he found that his master had crossed the river, knowing, too, that a great number of the troops had attempted to cross besides, and that, in all probability, many of them had succeeded in reaching the other bank, who would all be greatly in want of provisions and stores the next morning, he went to work at once, during the night, and loaded a very large boat with provisions, arms, money, and stuff to make clothing for the soldiers. He succeeded in getting off in this boat before his plan was discovered by the Monguls, and in the course of the next morning he reached the opposite bank with it, and thus furnished to Jalaloddin an abundant provision for his immediate necessities.

Jalaloddin was so much pleased with the conduct of Jamalarrazad in this affair that he appointed him at once to a very high and responsible office in his service, and gave him a new title of honor.

In the mean time, Genghis Khan, on the other side of the river, took possession the next morning of Jalaloddin's camp. Of course, the family of the sultan fell into his hands. The emperor ordered all the males to be killed, but he reserved the women for a different fate. Among the persons killed was a boy about eight years old, Jalaloddin's oldest son.

Jalaloddin had ordered his treasure to be sunk in the river, intending, probably, to come back and recover it at some future time. But Genghis Khan found out in some way where it was sunk, and he sent divers down for it, and thus obtained possession of it as a part of his booty.

After this, Jalaloddin remained five or six years in India, where he joined himself and his army with some of the princes of that country, and fought many campaigns there. At length, when a favorable opportunity occurred, he came back to his own country, and fought some time longer against the Monguls there, but he never succeeded in gaining possession of any substantial power.

Genghis Khan continued after this for two or three years in the Mohammedan countries of the western part of Asia, and extended his conquests there in every direction. It is not necessary to follow his movements in detail. It would only be a repetition of the same tale of rapine, plunder, murder, and devastation. Sometimes a city would surrender at once, when the conqueror approached the gates, by sending out a deputation of the magistrates and other principal inhabitants with the keys of the city, and with magnificent presents, in hopes to appease him. And they usually so far succeeded in this as to put the Mongul soldiery in good-humor, so that they would content themselves with ransacking and plundering the place, leaving the inhabitants alive. At other times the town would attempt to resist. The Monguls would then build engines to batter down the walls, and to hurl great stones over among the besieged. In many instances there was great difficulty in obtaining a sufficient supply of stones, on account of the alluvial character of the ground on which the city stood. In such cases, after the stones found near were exhausted, the besiegers would cut down great trees from the avenues leading to the town, or from the forests near, and, sawing the trunk up into short lengths, would use the immense blocks thus formed as ammunition for the engines. These great logs of heavy wood, when thrown over the walls, were capable of doing almost as much execution as the stones, though, compared with a modern bomb-shell—a monstrous ball of iron, which, after flying four or five miles from the battery, leaving on its way a fiery train through the air, descends into a town and bursts into a thousand fragments, which fly like iron hail in every direction around—they were very harmless missiles.

In sawing up the trunks of the trees into logs, and in bringing stones for the engines, the Monguls employed the prisoners whom they had taken in war and made slaves of. The amount of work of this kind which was to be done at some of the sieges was very great. It is said that at the siege of Nishabur—a town whose inhabitants greatly offended Genghis Khan by secretly sending arms, provisions, and money to Jalaloddin, after they had once surrendered to the Monguls and pretended to be friendly to them—the army of the Monguls employed twelve hundred of these engines, all of which were made at a town at some distance from the place besieged, and were then transported, in parts, by the slaves, and put together by them under the walls. While the slaves were employed in works of this kind, they were sometimes protected by wooden

145

shields covered with raw hides, which were carried before them by other slaves, to keep off and extinguish the fiery darts and arrows which were shot at them from the wall.

Sometimes, too, the places where the engines were set up were protected by wooden bulwarks, which, together with the frame-work itself of the engines, were covered with raw hides, to prevent their being set on fire by the enemy. The number of raw hides required for this purpose was immense, and to obtain them the Monguls slaughtered vast herds of horses and cattle which they plundered from the enemy.

In order to embarrass the enemy in respect to ammunition for their engines, the people of a town, when they heard that the Monguls were coming, used to turn out sometimes in mass, several days before, and gather up all the stones they could find, and throw them into the river, or otherwise put them out of the way.

In some cases, the towns that were threatened, as has already been said, did not attempt to resist, but submitted at once, and cast themselves on the mercy of the conqueror. In such cases the Mongul generals usually spared the lives of the inhabitants, though they plundered their property. It sometimes happened, too, that after attempting to defend themselves for some time, the garrison would become discouraged, and then would attempt to make some terms or conditions with the conqueror before they surrendered. In these cases, however, the terms which the Monguls insisted upon were often so hard that, rather than yield to them, the garrison would go on fighting to the end.

In one instance there lived in a town that was to be assailed a certain sheikh, or prince, named Kubru, who was a man of very exalted character, as well as of high distinction. The Mongul general whom Genghis Khan had commissioned to take the town was his third son, Oktay. Oktay had heard of the fame of the sheikh, and had conceived a very high respect for him. So he sent a herald to the wall with a passport for the sheikh, and for ten other persons such as he should choose, giving him free permission to leave the town and go wherever he pleased. But the sheikh declined the offer. Then Oktay sent in another passport, with permission to the sheikh to take a thousand men with him. But he still refused. He could not accept Oktay's bounty, he said, unless it were extended to all the Mohammedans in the town. He was obliged to take his lot with the rest, for he was bound to his people by ties too strong to be easily sundered.

So the siege went on, and at the end of it, when the town was carried, the sheikh was slain with the rest in the streets, where he stood his ground to the last, fighting like a lion.

All the Mohammedan chieftains, however, did not possess so noble a spirit as this. One chieftain, when he found that the Monguls were coming, caused himself to be let down with ropes from the wall in the night, and so made his escape, leaving the town and the garrison to their fate.

The garrisons of the towns, knowing that they had little mercy to expect from their terrible enemies, fought often very desperately to the last, as they would have done against beasts of prey. They would suddenly open the gates and rush out in large bands, provided with combustibles of all kinds and torches, with which they would set fire to the engines of the besiegers, and then get back again within the walls before the Monguls could recover sufficiently from the alarm and confusion to intercept them. In this manner they destroyed a great many of the engines, and killed vast numbers of men.

Still the Monguls would persevere, and, sooner or later, the place was sure to fall. Then, when the inhabitants found that all hope was over, they had become so desperate in their hatred of their foes that they would sometimes set the town on fire with their own hands, and throw themselves and their wives and children into the flames, rather than fall into the hands of their infuriated enemies.

The cruelties which the Monguls perpetrated upon their unhappy victims when, after a long resistance, they finally gained possession of a town, were indeed dreadful. They usually ordered all the people to come out to an open space on the plain, and there, after taking out all the young and able-bodied men, who could be made useful in bringing stones and setting up engines, and other such labors, and also all the young and beautiful women, to be divided among the army or sold as slaves, they would put the rest together in a mass, and kill them all by shooting at them with arrows, just as if they had been beasts surrounded in a chase, excepting that the excitement and pleasure of shooting into such a mass of human victims, and of hearing the shrieks and cries of their terror, was probably infinitely greater to their brutal murderers than if it had been a herd of lions, tigers, and wolves that they were destroying.

It is said by the historians that in one case the number of people ordered out upon the plain was so great that it took four days for them to pass out and assemble at the appointed place, and that, after those who were to be spared had been separated from the rest, the number that were left to be slain was over one hundred thousand, as recorded by the secretaries who made an enumeration of them.

In another case the slaughter was so great that it took twelve days to count the number of the dead.

Some of the atrocities which were perpetrated upon the prisoners were almost too horrible to be described. In one case a woman, quite advanced in years, begged the Monguls to spare her life, and promised that, if they would do so, she would give them a pearl of great value.

147

They asked her where the pearl was, and she said she had swallowed it. The Monguls then immediately cut her down, and ripped her body open with their swords to find the pearl. They found it, and then, encouraged by this success, and thinking it probable that other women might have attempted to hide their jewels in the same way, they proceeded to kill and cut open a great number of women to search for pearls in their bodies, but they found no more.

At the siege of a certain city, called Bamiyan, a young grandson of Genghis Khan, wishing to please his grandfather by his daring, approached so near the wall that he was reached by an arrow shot by one of the archers, and killed. Genghis Khan was deeply affected by this event, and he showed by the bitterness of his grief that, though he was so utterly heartless and cruel in inflicting these woes upon others, he could feel for himself very acutely when it came to his turn to suffer. As for the mother of the child, she was rendered perfectly furious by his death. She thought of nothing but revenge, and she only waited for the town to be taken in order that she might enjoy it. When, at last, a practicable breach was made, and the soldiers began to pour into the city, she went in with the rest, and insisted that every man, woman, and child should be put to death. Her special rage was directed against the children, whom she seemed to take special pleasure in destroying, in vengeance for the death of her own child. The hatred and rage which she manifested against children extended even to babes unborn, and these feelings she evinced by atrocities too shocking to be described.

The opinions which Genghis Khan entertained on religious subjects appear from a conversation which he held at one time during the course of his campaigns in Western Asia with some learned Mohammedan doctors at Bokhara, which was the great seat at that time of science and philosophy. He asked the doctors what were the principles of their religion. They replied that these principles consisted of five fundamental points:

1. In believing in one God, the creator of all things, and   the supreme ruler and governor of the universe.
2. In giving one fortieth part of their yearly income or   gains to the poor.
3. In praying to God five times every day.
4. In setting apart one month in each year for fasting.
5. In making a pilgrimage to the temple in Mecca, there to   worship God.

Genghis Khan told them that he believed himself in the first of these articles, and he approved of the three succeeding ones. It was very well, he said, to give one fortieth of one's income to the poor, and to pray to God five times a day, and to set apart a month in the year for a fast. But as to the last article, he could not

148

but dissent from it entirely, for the whole world was God's house, and it was ridiculous, he said, to imagine that one place could really be any more fitting than another as a place for worshiping him.

The learned doctors were much dissatisfied with this answer. They were, in fact, more displeased with the dissent which the emperor expressed from this last article, the only one that was purely and wholly ritual in its character, than they were gratified with the concurrence which he expressed in all the other four. This is not at all surprising, for, from the times of the Pharisees down to the present day, the spirit of sectarianism and bigotry in religion always plants itself most strongly on the platform of externals. It is always contending strenuously for rites, while it places comparatively in the background all that bears directly on the vital and spiritual interests of the soul.

CHAPTER 23: GRAND CELEBRATIONS
1221-1224

The great hunting party—Object of the hunt—The general plan—The time arrives—Orders—Progress of the operations—Terror of the animals—The inner circle—Condition of the beasts—The princes enter the ring—Intimidation of the wild beasts—They recover their ferocity when attacked—The slaughter—Petition of the young men—End of the hunt—The assembly at Toukat—Return of Genghis Khan's sons—Present of horses—The khans arrive—Grand entertainment—Drinks—Great extent of the encampment—Laying out the encampment—The state tent—The throne—Business transacted—Leave-taking—The assembly is dismissed.

When Genghis Khan found that his conquests in Western Asia were in some good degree established and confirmed, he illustrated his victory and the consequent extension of his empire by two very imposing celebrations. The first was a grand hunt. The second was a solemn convocation of all the estates of his immense realm in a sort of diet or deliberative assembly.

The accounts given by the historians of both these celebrations are doubtless greatly exaggerated. Their description of the hunt is as follows:

It was after the close of the campaign in 1221 that it took place, while the army were in winter quarters. The object of the hunt was to keep the soldiers occupied, so as to avoid the relaxation of discipline, and the vices and disorder which generally creep into a camp where there are no active occupations to engage the minds of the men. The hunt took place in a vast region of uninhabited country, which was infested with wild beasts of every kind. The soldiers were marched out on this expedition in order of war, as if it were a country occupied by armed men that they were going to attack. The different detachments were conducted to the different points in the outskirts of the country, from which they severally extended themselves to the right and left, so as completely to inclose the ground. And the space was so large, it is said, which was thus inclosed, that it took them several weeks to march in to the centre.

It is true that in such a case the men would advance very slowly, perhaps only a few miles each day, in order that they might examine the ground thoroughly, and leave no ravine, or thicket, or other lurking-place, where beasts might conceal themselves, unexplored. Still, the circle was doubtless immensely large.

When the appointed morning at length arrived, the men at the several stations were arrayed, and they commenced their advance toward the centre, moving to the sound of trumpets, drums, timbrels, and other such instruments of martial music as were in use in those days.

The men were strictly forbidden to kill any animal. They were only to start them out from their lurking-places and lairs, and drive them in toward the centre of the field.

Great numbers of the men were provided with picks, spades, and other similar tools, with which they were to dig out the burrows and holes of such animals as should seek refuge underground.

They went on in this way for some weeks. The animals ran before them, thinking, when they were disturbed by the men, that it was only a momentary danger, which they could easily escape from, as usual, by running forward into the next thicket; but soon the advancing line of the soldiers reached them there, and drove them out again, and if they attempted to turn to the right or the left they soon found themselves intercepted. Thus, as the circle grew narrower, and the space inclosed diminished, the animals began to find themselves mixing with one another in great numbers, and being now irritated and angry, they attacked one another in many instances, the strong falling upon and killing the weak. Thus a great many were killed, though not by the hands of the soldiers.

At last the numbers became so great, and the excitement and terror of the animals so intense, that the soldiers had great difficulty in driving them forward. The poor beasts ran this way and that, half distracted, while the soldiers pressed steadily on behind them, and cut them off from every chance of escape by raising terrific shouts and outcries, and by brandishing weapons before them wherever they attempted to turn.

At length the animals were all driven in to the inner circle, a comparatively small space, which had been previously marked out. Around this space double and triple lines of troops were drawn up, armed with pikes and spears, which they pointed in toward the centre, thus forming a sort of wall by which the beasts were closely shut in. The plan was now for the officers and khans, and all the great personages of the court and the army, to go into the circle, and show their courage and their prowess by attacking the beasts and slaying them.

But the courage required for such an exploit was not so great as it might seem, for it was always found on these occasions that the beasts, though they had been very wild and ferocious when first aroused from their lairs, and had appeared excessively irritated when they found the circle beginning to narrow around them, ended at last in losing all their spirit, and in becoming discouraged, dejected, and tame. This was owing partly, perhaps, to their having become, in

151

some degree, familiar with the sight of men, but more probably to the exhaustion produced by long-continued fatigue and excitement, and to their having been for so many days deprived in a great degree of their accustomed food and rest.

Thus in this, as in a great many other similar instances, the poor soldiers and common people incurred the danger and the toil, and then the great men came in at the end to reap the glory.

Genghis Khan himself was the first to enter the circle for the purpose of attacking the beasts. He was followed by the princes of his family, and by other great chieftains and khans. As they went in, the whole army surrounded the inclosure, and completely filled the air with the sound of drums, timbrels, trumpets, and other such instruments, and with the noise of the most terrific shouts and outcries which they could make, in order to terrify and overawe the beasts as much as possible, and to destroy in them all thought and hope of resistance.

And, indeed, so much effect was produced by these means of intimidation, that the beasts, it is said, became completely stupefied. "They were so affrighted that they lost all their fierceness. The lions and tigers became as tame as lambs, and the bears and wild boars, like the most timorous creatures, became dejected and amazed."

Still, the going in of Genghis Khan and the princes to attack them was not wholly without danger; for, of course, it was a point of honor with them to select the most ferocious and fierce of the animals, and some of these, when they found themselves actually assailed, were aroused again, and, recovering in some degree their native ferocity, seemed impelled to make a last desperate effort to defend themselves. After killing a few of the lions, tigers, and bears, Genghis Khan and his immediate suite retired to a place at one side of the inclosure, where a throne had been set up for the emperor on an eminence which afforded a good view of the field. Here Genghis Khan took his seat in order to enjoy the spectacle of the slaughter, and then an immense number of men were allowed to go in and amuse themselves with killing and destroying the poor beasts till they were perfectly satiated with the sight of blood and of suffering.

At last some of the khan's grandsons, attended by several other young princes, approached the throne where the emperor was seated, and petitioned him to order the carnage to cease, and to allow the rest of the animals to go free. This petition the emperor granted. The lines were broken up, the animals that had escaped being massacred made their way back into the wilds again, and the hunt was over.

The several detachments of the army then set out on their march back to the camp again. But so great was the scale on which this grand hunting expedition was conducted, that four months elapsed between the time of their setting out upon it till the time of their return.

*   *   *   *   *

The grand diet or general assembly of the states of Genghis Khan's empire took place two or three years later, when the conquest of Western Asia was complete, and the sons of the emperor and all the great generals could be called together at the emperor's head-quarters without much danger. The place chosen for this assembly was a vast plain in the vicinity of the city of Toukat, which has already been mentioned as one of the great cities conquered by Genghis Khan. Toukat lay in a central and convenient position for the purpose of this assembly. It was, moreover, a rich and beautiful city, and could furnish all that would be necessary for the wants of the assembly. The meeting, however, was not to be held in the city itself, but upon a great plain in the environs of it, where there was space for all the khans, with their numerous retinues, to pitch their tents.

When the khans and chieftains began to assemble, there came first the sons of the king, returning from the various expeditions on which their father had sent them, and bringing with them magnificent presents. These presents, of course, consisted of the treasures and other valuables which they had taken in plunder from the various cities which had fallen into their hands. The presents which Jughi brought exceeded in value those of all the others. Among the rest, there was a herd of horses one hundred thousand in number. These horses had, of course, been seized in the pastures of the conquered countries, and were now brought to the emperor to be used by him in mounting his troops. They were arrayed in bands according to the color, white, dappled gray, bay, black, and spotted, of each kind an equal number.

The emperor received and welcomed his sons with great joy, and readily accepted their presents. In return, he made presents to them from his own treasuries.

After this, as other princes and khans came in, and encamped with their troops and followers on the plain, the emperor entertained them all with a series of grand banquets and public diversions of all sorts. Among other things a grand hunting party was organized, somewhat similar in the general plan to the one already described, only on a much smaller scale, of course, in respect to the number of persons engaged and the time occupied, while yet it greatly surpassed that one in magnificence and splendor. Several thousand beasts were slain, it is said, and a great number and variety of birds, which were taken by the falcons.

153

At the end of the hunt a great banquet was given, which surpassed all the other feasts in munificence. They had on the tables of this banquet a great variety of drinks—not only rich wines from the southern countries, but beer, and metheglin, and also sherbet, which the army had learned to make in Persia.

In the mean time, the great space on the plain, which had been set apart for the encampment, had been gradually becoming filled up by the arrival of the khans, until at length, in every direction, as far as the eye could reach, the whole plain was covered with groups of tents and long lines of movable houses, brought on wheels. The ground which the encampment covered was said by the historians to have been seven leagues in extent. If the space occupied was anything at all approaching this magnitude, it could only be that the outer portions of it were occupied by the herdsmen and other servants of the khans, who had to take care of the cattle and horses of the troops, and to provide them with suitable pasture. Indeed, the great number of animals which these wandering tribes always took with them on their journeys rendered it necessary to appropriate a much larger space to their encampments than would have been otherwise required.

It is surprising to us, who are accustomed to look upon living in tents as so exclusively an irregular and temporary expedient, to learn how completely this mode of life was reduced to a system in those days, and how perfect and complete all the arrangements relating to it were made. In this case, in the centre of the encampment, a space of two leagues in length was regularly laid out in streets, squares, and market-places, like a town. Here were the emperor's quarters, with magnificent tents for himself and his immediate household, and multitudes of others of a plainer character for his servants and retainers. The tents of the other grand khans were near. They were made of rich materials, and ornamented in a sumptuous manner, and silken streamers of various colors floated in the wind from the summits of them.

Besides these there was an immense tent, built for the assembly itself to hold its sessions in. This tent was so large, it is said, that it would contain two thousand persons. It was covered with white, which made it very conspicuous. There were two entrance-gates leading to the interior. One of them was called the imperial gate, and was for the use of Genghis Khan alone. The other was the public gate, and was used in general for the members of the assembly and for spectators.

Within the tent was erected a magnificent throne, intended for the use of the emperor during the sessions of the assembly.

A great amount of important business was transacted by the assembly while it continued in session, and many important edicts were made by the emperor. The constitution and laws of the empire were promulgated anew, and all necessary arrangements made for the government of the various provinces both near and remote.

At length, when these various objects had been accomplished, and the business was concluded, the emperor gave audience individually to all the princes, khans, generals, governors of provinces, and other grand dignitaries who were present on the occasion, in order that they might take their leave preparatory to returning to their several countries. When this ceremony was concluded the encampment was broken up, and the various khans set off, each at the head of his own caravan, on the road leading to his own home.

CHAPTER 24: CONCLUSION
1227

Death of the khan's oldest son—Effects of this calamity—Plan for the invasion of China—The khan's sons—His sickness—Change for the worse—Farewell address—He claims the right to name his successor—Other arrangements—Death of the emperor—His grave and monument—Visits of condolence to the new emperor—Fate of the empire.

After the grand convocation described in the last chapter, Genghis Khan lived only three years. During this time he went on extending his conquests with the same triumphant success that had attended his previous operations. Having at length established his dominion in Western Asia on a permanent basis, he returned to the original seat of his empire in the East, after seven years' absence, where he was received with great honor by the Mongul nation. He began again to extend his conquests in China. He was very successful. Indeed, with the exception of one great calamity which befell him, his career was one of continued and unexampled prosperity.

This calamity was the death of his son Jughi, his oldest, most distinguished, and best-beloved son. The news of this event threw the khan into a deep melancholy, so that for a time he lost all his interest in public affairs, and even the news of victories obtained in distant countries by his armies ceased to awaken any joyful emotions in his mind.

The khan was now, too, becoming quite advanced in life, being about sixty-four years old, which is an age at which the mind is slow to recover its lost elasticity. He did, however, slowly recover from the effects of his grief, and he then went on with his warlike preparations. He had conquered all the northern portion of China, and was now making arrangements for a grand invasion of the southern part, when at length, in the spring of the year 1227, he fell sick. He struggled against the disease during the summer, but at length, in August, he found himself growing worse, and felt that his end was drawing nigh.

His mind was occupied mainly, during all this interval, by arranging the details of the coming campaign, and making known to the officers around him all the particulars of his plans, in order that they might carry them out successfully after his decease. He was chiefly concerned, as well he might be, lest the generals should quarrel among each other after he should be gone, and he continually exhorted them to be united, and on no account to allow discord or dissensions to creep in and divide them.

His oldest son, next to Jughi, was Jagatay, but he was of a mild and amiable temper, and not so well qualified to govern so widely-extended an empire as the next son, whose name was Oktay. The next son to Oktay, whose name was Toley, was with his father at the time when his sickness at last assumed an immediately alarming character.

This change for the worse, which convinced the emperor that his death was drawing nigh, took place one day when he was traveling with a portion of his army, being borne on a litter on account of his infirm and feeble condition. A halt was ordered, a camp was formed, and the great conqueror was borne to a tent which was pitched for him on the spot near the borders of the forest. The physicians and the astrologers came around him, and tried to comfort him with encouraging predictions, but he knew by the pains that he felt, and by other inward sensations, that his hour had come.

He accordingly ordered that all of his sons who were in the camp, and all the princes of his family, should be called in to his bedside. When they had all assembled, he caused himself to be raised up in his bed, and then made a short but very solemn address to them.

"I leave you," said he, "the greatest empire in the world, but your preserving it depends upon your remaining always united. If discord steals in among you all will most assuredly be lost."

Then, turning to the great chieftains and khans who were standing by—the great nobles of his court—he appealed to them, as well as to the princes of his family, whether it was not just and reasonable that he, who had established the empire, and built it up wholly from the very foundations, should have the right to name a successor to inherit it after he was gone.

They all expressed a full assent to this proposition. His sons and the other princes of his family fell on their knees and said, "You are our father and our emperor, and we are your slaves. It is for us to bow in submission to all the commands with which you honor us, and to render the most implicit obedience to them."

The khan then proceeded to announce to the assembly that he had made choice of his son Oktay as his successor, and he declared him the khan of khans, which was the imperial title, according to the constitution.

The whole assembly then kneeled again, and solemnly declared that they accepted the choice which the emperor had made, and promised allegiance and fidelity to the new sovereign so soon as he should be invested with power.

The aged emperor then gave to his second son, Jagatay, a large country for his kingdom, which, however, he was, of course, to hold under the general sovereignty of his brother. He also appointed his son Toley, who was then present, to act as regent until Oktay should return.

The assembly was then dismissed, and very soon afterward the great conqueror died.

Toley, of course, immediately entered upon his office as regent, and under his direction the body of his father was interred, with great magnificence, under a venerable tree, where the khan had rested himself with great satisfaction a few days before he was taken sick.

The spot was a very beautiful one, and in due time a magnificent monument was erected over the grave. Trees were afterward planted around the spot, and other improvements were made in the grounds, by which it became, at length, it was said, one of the finest sepulchres in the world.

As soon as Oktay, whom the emperor had designated as his successor, returned home, he was at once proclaimed emperor, and established himself at his father's court. The news of the old emperor's death rapidly spread throughout Asia, and a succession of ambassadors were sent from all the provinces, principalities, and kingdoms throughout the empire, and also from such contiguous states as desired to maintain friendly relations with the new monarch, to bring addresses and messages of condolence from their respective rulers. And so great was the extent of country from which these ambassadors came that a period of six months was consumed before these melancholy ceremonies were ended.

*   *   *   *   *

The fate of the grand empire which Genghis Khan established was the same with that of all others that have arisen in the world, from time to time, by the extension of the power of great military commanders over widely-separated and heterogeneous nations. The sons and successors to whom the vast possessions descended soon quarreled among themselves, and the immense fabric fell to pieces in less time than it had taken to construct it.

THE END.

Printed in Great Britain
by Amazon

27457055R00089